'I PERCEIVE
THAT IN ALL
THINGS YE
ARE TOO
SUPERSTITIOUS.'

ACTS 17:22

SUPERSTITIONS
PETER HAINING

TREASURE PRESS

ACKNOWLEDGEMENTS

For Bernard and Bridget – with fingers crossed!

The author and publishers are grateful to those listed below for supplying and/or giving permission to reproduce the illustrations on the pages given. All other illustrations were supplied by the author from his private collection.

Michael Busselle (P.H.), page 168 bottom.

Camera Press, 172

Mary Evans Picture Library, 15 top, 24, 30–1, 45 (2), 48, 53, 54, 58, 62, 67, 72, 84 bottom, 87, 100 top, 107, 111, 112, 113, 114, 118 bottom, 124 bottom, 150, 151.

National Film Archive (P.H.), 34, 167.

P.A.–Reuter Photos Ltd (P.H.), 137.

Photopress (P.H.), 13 bottom.

Popperfoto, 11, 12, 14, 25 top, 32 bottom, 49, 64–5, 108, 109, 110, 118 top, 120, 130, 143, 152, 156.

Eileen Ramsay (P.H.), 144 bottom.

Rank Film Distributors Limited (P.H.), 88.

Rex Features Ltd, 15 bottom (Agence Dalmas), 16 (photo Bill Orchard), 20 (photo Bill Orchard), 25 bottom (photo Dave M. Enery), 27 (2), 28 (photo G. Sipahioglu), 29 (Agence Dalmas), 57, 59 (photo Felix Fonteyn), 70 (A. Devaney Inc.), 98–9, 122 (Grazia Neri), 145 (Pierluigi), 146–7, 154 (Fotopress).

R.K.O. Pictures Ltd (P.H.), 44.

B.P. Singer Features Inc. (P.H.), 36, 124 top.

Theatre Advertising Co. (P.H.), 75.

A.C.K. Ware (P.H.), 84 top.

West Essex Gazette (P.H.), 125.

First published in Great Britain in 1979 by Sidgwick and Jackson Limited

This edition published in 1990 by Treasure Press
Michelin House
81 Fulham Road
London SW3 6RB

Copyright © 1979 Peter Haining and Sidgwick and Jackson Limited

ISBN 1-85051-463-1

Printed in Portugal

Designed by John Riley

Picture research by Peter Haining and Annie Horton

Page 2: One of Gustave Doré's illustrations for Coleridge's famous poem of superstition at sea, *The Ancient Mariner*, first published in 1798

Page 3: Dwarfs and hunchbacks have long been considered good luck for gamblers

CONTENTS

CHAPTER 1

THE WORLD OF THE SUPERSTITIOUS

The Scandinavian god Loki, who caused the death of the beloved Balder at a gathering of thirteen people and gave rise to the bad luck associated with this number. From an old manuscript in the Royal Library, Copenhagen

Vatican affirms existence of the devil

Rome, June 25.—The Vatican today reaffirmed that the devil exists. The assertion was made in a two-page supplement to the Vatican newspaper *L'Osservatore Romano*, in which an expert of the Sacred Congregation for the Doctrine of the Faith, formerly known as the Holy Office, traced the history of the church's attitude to demonology over the centuries.

"The existence of the devil's world is revealed as a fact of dogma in the Gospel", the article said. It was "a central tenet of the faith of the church and of its conception of redemption".

Contemporary studies by scholars and theologians casting doubt on the existence of the devil "could not but trouble people's souls", the article added.—Reuter.

The Devil alive and well – a report from *The Times*, 25 June 1978

So you think you're not superstitious?

It is a natural enough reaction to deny giving any sort of credence to beliefs that are undeniably steeped in mystery, cluttered with elements of the unknown, and often rooted in the illogical and the inexplicable. Yet I suspect the reaction is one half of embarrassment, half of bravado: for it it were truly the case you would not even be reading this book, would you?

The degree to which we are governed by superstitious beliefs varies. Some of us may get by with no more than half a dozen, surreptitiously practised when we think no one is looking; others may observe each omen, watch for every sign, and avoid any action which somehow puts them in danger of the unknown. For it *is* fear of the unknown, surely one of man's primary instincts, which lies at the very heart of superstition: the reason why even in our advanced scientific and technological society customs as old as man himself survive, some unchanged, others altering almost uncannily to keep pace with the times. When we are in any way anxious, when tension surrounds some part of our lives, and when we could use a little good luck or ward off some misfortune, then superstition with its roots in ancient magic insinuates itself unbidden into our thoughts.

Margaret Mead, the distinguished American anthropologist, in her important study, *Growth and Culture* (1951), tells us that 'superstition has been a part of every civilization's culture' and she has demonstrated how, from his days as a savage, man has observed these beliefs in one form or another. The forces of nature surrounded him, and he read much into the portents of the skies, into the actions of birds, animals and insects, not to mention his own body and the intimate affairs of his daily existence. Demons and spirits were believed to operate many of these superstitions, yet when civilization dawned, and after it came the march of progress, nothing could shift the darkness of the unknown that was indelibly printed on the human psyche. Early man saw everything around him as controlled by supernatural forces, and wanted somehow to utilize this 'magic' (for superstition is closely related to magic) as a form of control over the natural world in which he lived.

The word superstition is derived from the Latin *superstitio* which means super, above, and *state*, to stand. (In the days of hand to hand fighting those who survived the conflict were known as 'superstites' – that is they were 'standing above' the slain.) From this has derived the meaning that it indicates standing over something in amazement. Yet dictionaries nowadays – and I take *Chamber's Twentieth Century Dictionary* as a typical example – are emphatic in their dismissal of the implications:

Superstition, false worship or religion; an ignorant and irrational belief in supernatural agency, omens, divination, sorcery, etc: a deep-rooted but unfounded general belief: a rite or practice proceeding from superstitious belief or fear.

Such a definite viewpoint, however, seems to me to ignore one of the most important points about man: that he is partly an irrational creature, and that many of his greatest achievements in science, philosophy and religion have stemmed from his irrationality. Superstition, too, is a development of this attitude of mind and has given rise to it being described as a 'half belief', as Douglas Hill explains in his book, *Magic and Superstition* (1968):

The traditional concept of the 'father' of superstitions, the Devil. An eighteenth-century French engraving

THE WORLD OF THE SUPERSTITIOUS

William Shakespeare was a superstitious man and made much use of omens in his work

A British psychologist, Peter McKellar, has used the term 'half belief' for this widespread attitude – the half-believers, seeing themselves as rational beings, will intellectually reject superstition, and thus will claim that they carry a rabbit's foot just for the fun of it, or that they touch wood as a joke. But that they perform these actions is all revealing. Somehow they are playing safe, hedging their bets, refusing entirely to reject the possibility that there might be 'something in it' after all, that luck may be in some way controllable. We may not be as superstition-dominated as our ancestors; but as long as this propensity to an irrational half-belief exists, the old wives' tales, the omens and taboos and rituals will continue to find fertile growing ground.

A recent report has gone even further than this and suggested that despite all our sophistication, superstition is today actually undergoing a renaissance unequalled since the Middle Ages. The man behind this claim is Dr Howard Tills, a retired Cambridge professor and a leading authority on superstition. He believes people are even more superstitious now than they were at the beginning of the century, probably because of the increasing uncertainty of the times. And, he goes on, he believes superstition does have a tendency to work, 'because it is belief operating at its most potent level, that of the sub-conscious. In modern jargon, it is mind conditioning.'

Dr Tills claims that a firmly held superstition can be as therapeutic as a psychiatrist, more reliable than a computer. 'If a man or woman performs some odd little act because they think it will bring them luck, then the chances are that it will do so because the layers of self-doubt which inhibit so many of our actions have been seeded with positive thought.'

If we have cause to doubt the statements of men like McKellar and Tills, it is only really necessary to look at the weight of facts and figures that exist about the impact of superstition over the years to become aware of the role it has played in human history. For we know a good deal not only about those who admitted to being superstitious but also about the superstitions in which they believed and how they affected their lives.

History is replete with stories of famous people who were superstitious, for as Shakespeare – a prominent member of that order – has observed:

There is a tide in the affairs of men,
Which, taken at the flood, leads on to fortune.

As we shall see throughout this book, the Greeks and Romans were plagued by fear of the unknown and inspired a great many superstitions, and even the famous Socrates was constantly nervous about presuming on the fates. Alexander the Great, too, fell

Christopher Columbus had to fight off superstition during his perilous voyage to discover America

prey to superstition and a contributory factor to his early death was undoubtedly the prediction by his priests that seizing Babylon would prove fatal. That ill-omened man, Julius Caesar, read portents in the stars of his forthcoming death, while it was only quick thinking and a thorough knowledge of superstition that enabled William the Conqueror to convince his followers that their mission was not doomed when he stumbled on landing on the English shore: for such an event was supposed to presage disaster. Christopher Columbus had to fight superstition all the way to the new world, for his men believed the sharks which dogged their vessel were an omen of disaster, and he called on the old custom of hurling a pack of playing cards into the ocean during a terrible storm in order to quell the waves.

Queen Elizabeth II is just one of many Royals to have shown due consideration to old superstitions over the years

Royalty, too, has been influenced by superstition, and King Henry VIII was convinced that witchcraft had made him fall in love with Anne Boleyn, while both Charles I and James II were certain they read signs of their unhappy fates in the skies. And superstition credited kings with having the special gift of a touch which enabled them to cure 'the King's evil', scrofula, by merely placing their hands on a sufferer's head. Despite all her rationality, Queen Elizabeth I placed great store by fortune-telling, and that pillar of mortality, Queen Victoria, was not above sending a charm to ward off evil when her favourite minister, Lord Melbourne, lay ill. Our present Queen, Elizabeth II, also showed she was superstitious recently when she insisted on handing over a

Dr Samuel Johnson was prey to all manner of superstitions – and what would he have thought of having his picture appear on page 13 of a book!

halfpenny in return for a gift of cutlery – for to receive knives without a payment of some kind is to risk 'cutting' the ties of friendship. And the Duke of Edinburgh admits he always gives his polo helmet seven ceremonial taps for luck before beginning a game.

Even in the world of letters superstition has made itself evident. Shakespeare's works are full of instances showing how well versed he was in old beliefs, and he particularly believed that sleeping in a bed that was over four hundred years old contributed to his success. Dr Samuel Johnson always walked out of a door with his right foot first, believed he could ensure good luck by touching every wooden post he passed, and *never* walked on the cracks between paving stones. The poet Byron believed Friday was an unlucky day, yet defied his conviction to sail from Italy on this day – and died not long after . . . on a Friday. I also recently heard that Graham Greene cannot bring himself to write a word until a particular antique ink well is sitting on his desk and he has rubbed it a couple of times for luck.

Winston Churchill was another person who believed Friday was an ill-omened day and did not like travelling then; if forced to do so, he took his 'lucky' walking stick. He also delighted in stroking black cats, and among the very superstitious this is said to have given him the good luck needed to win the Second World War.

Right: Sir Winston Churchill with his 'lucky' walking stick – one of several superstitions observed by this great English statesman

Left: The Duke of Edinburgh always taps his polo helmet seven times for good luck before beginning a game

Both Hitler and Mussolini were greatly influenced by superstition. Hitler particularly believed in the power of the number seven, while Mussolini was terrified of the 'Evil Eye'

The two dictators, Adolf Hitler and Benito Mussolini, were perhaps not surprisingly very much in awe of superstition: Mussolini nursed a fear of the 'Evil Eye' all his life and would change places rather than sit next to anyone he felt possessed this sinister influence. Hitler, for his part, believed in the mystic power of the number seven and constantly sought advice from astrologers before planning his next course of action.

Perhaps the most unnerving of all superstitions concerning the famous deals with the office of President of the United States of America. For ever since the year 1840 there has been a belief that each president elected at twenty-year intervals thereafter will die in office. The record proves that this is just what has happened.

THE WORLD OF THE SUPERSTITIOUS

Abraham Lincoln – just one American President to fall victim to a superstition which haunts that high office

John F. Kennedy and his family. He was the most recent American President to die in office, thereby continuing an uncanny superstitious prophecy

The man who instigated this grim chain was William Henry Harrison who was elected in 1840 and died while still holding the post. Then came Abraham Lincoln (1809–1865) who was elected in 1860 and actually observed, 'I feel a presentiment that I shall not outlast the rebellion. When it is over my work will be done.' With uncanny prophecy the superstition continued with James A. Garfield (1831–1881) who was elected in 1880, William McKinley (1843–1901) elected in 1900, Warren G. Harding (1865–1923) elected in 1920, Franklin D. Roosevelt (1882–1945) elected in 1940, and finally John F. Kennedy (1917–1963) elected in 1960. The next test for this strange superstition will fall on whoever is elected in 1980.

While the famous have left us documentation of their superstition, there have been uncounted millions of ordinary people who have clung to similar beliefs. The strength of their belief is evidenced by the vast array of superstitions we still have today.

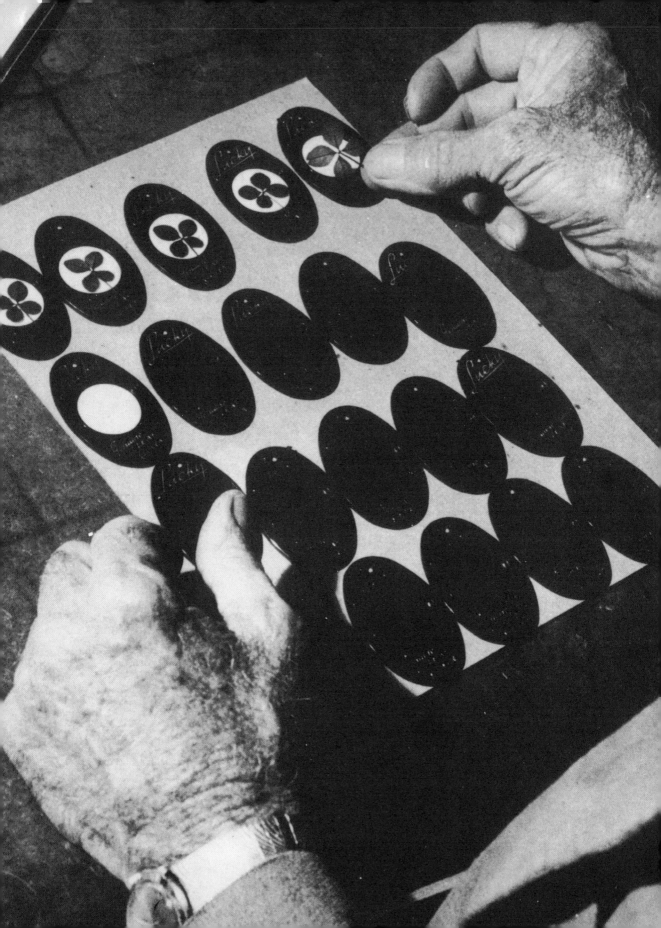

COM-MANDING OIL

A blend of special ingredients alleged to produce a commanding scent that will be appealing to those in love. (2 dram bottle)

HI JOHN CONQUEROR OIL

Made with a herb known as John the Conqueror Root, believed by many to create good luck in love and money matters. (2 dram bottle)

FAST LUCK POWDER

Alleged to bring good luck to those who use it. Made from the finest ingredients obtainable. Our trade mark for this aromatic sachet. (1 oz. jar)

PLANE-TARY PERFUME

A different scent represents the flower of your birth month. Believed by many to create a harmonious vibration for those who use it. Be sure and give Birthdate.

Superstition is now a good commercial proposition, as these preparations indicate

Superstition as big business – four-leaf clovers being mounted for sale as good luck charms. Many thousands of these are sold each year.

One thing that has occurred in this century has been the first determined effort to try and discover through surveys just how large a percentage of the ·general public *do* admit to being superstitious. The startling conclusion from each succeeding survey has been that the percentage is constantly growing!

In the first, and still one of the most important surveys, in 1907, Professor Fletcher Dressler of the University of California found in a group of 875 students that almost 45 per cent believed in superstition to some extent; in 1921 Professor Russell Gould, at Edinburgh University, polled a similar number of students and got an estimate of 48 per cent who were unable to deny some belief. By 1933 the Maller and Lundeen Survey showed the percentage was over the 50 per cent mark, while the continuing work in this field by the American Dr Otis W. Caldwell in the thirties and forties led him to admit shortly before his death in 1947 that he believed somewhere in the region of 90 per cent of the people in the United States were influenced to some degree by superstition. The recent work of Iona and Peter Opie among schoolchildren in the British Isles has shown how children have continued to pick up superstitions, and while many of them have thought such things were 'silly' only when it was pointed out how many of the beliefs they took for granted were actually superstitions did they appreciate that the ideas were just as firmly rooted in their minds as they had been with their parents. An interesting fact underlined by all these surveys is that more females than males believed in superstition. Among girls and boys the percentages ran fairly close at 20 to 25 per cent, while 60 per cent of adult women admitted to a belief as against 40 per cent of men. Of course, one must always allow for reticence and similar factors in such surveys, but the figures are nonetheless interesting. The more recent surveys also seem to have disproved the idea that it was the poorer or working-class people who were more prone to superstitions than any other group: in fact superstition seems to grip anyone who feels insecure, whatever his social background.

The impact of superstition on our world can also be judged in commercial terms, for it was estimated a short while ago that about 10 million rabbits' feet are sold in America every year, and about half that number in Europe. In the British Isles something like a million four-leafed clovers are bought each year, while the figure is almost trebled across the Atlantic. I have also seen it reported that Americans spend in excess of $125 million on various forms of fortune-telling and divination, and the figure in Britain and Europe must certainly exceed the million pound mark. Taken together, the best-selling good luck charms are black cats,

Two of the most popular good luck charms, Joan the Wad and Jack O'Lantern, based on little creatures from English West Country superstitions

horseshoes, rabbits' feet and white heather. Irish leprechauns and Cornish piskies have been very popular for generations, and of late are being joined in the popularity stakes by Joan the Wad and Jack O'Lantern, who are male and female aspects of Ignis Fatuus, the fire spirit of the Fens. (I should perhaps note that there is also a flourishing industry manufacturing witchcraft equipment, including printed Magic Circles, Ritual Knives and all the other accoutrements of this practice.)

As a result of all this recent study, it is now possible to state with some assurance which are the world's four most popular good luck and bad luck superstitions. To take the good luck first: by far the most widely practised is the custom of 'touching' or 'knocking on' wood. This is followed by 'wishing on a star', belief in the good fortune inherent in finding a four-leafed clover, and, fourthly, the protection offered by a horseshoe. Heading the bad luck list are black cats (the British are, in fact, almost the only nation to consider them lucky), the misfortune incurred by breaking a mirror, the number thirteen and, finally, walking under a ladder.

Perhaps, here, I may elaborate a little on these to familiarize you with the style adopted to discuss all the other superstitions recounted in this book. It has been my intention, as you will see, not only to discuss those beliefs which are still most universally known and practised, but also to explain wherever possible how they originated, although this is often difficult because so many belong to the very earliest times long before records of any kind

The good luck of the four-leaf clover utilized as a sales device by a Chicago store. From *The Sunday Bulletin*, 6 November 1977

Good luck in abundance – a field of four-leaf clovers. The actual location is kept a well-guarded secret by the owners!

were kept. What has been interesting to find is how many of the oldest superstitions have survived almost unchanged, sometimes transported continents apart, and that so-called 'new' superstitions are really only variations on much older ones. Eric Maple, the folklorist and author who was responsible for sparking my early interest in the supernatural, has put it very succinctly in his book, *Superstition and the Superstitious* (1971): 'There are apparently no absolutely new superstitions but only ancient ones which, as if possessed by some diabolical instinct for survival, persist in advancing from generation to generation disguised as novelties.'

But to get to the most popular good luck superstitions, beginning with 'touching wood'. This action of touching or knocking on the nearest piece of wood is invariably associated with some boasting or optimistic remark and is instinctive for fear of offending the fates and jeopardizing whatever it is that is wished for. It has been suggested that the origin of this belief stems from the time when early Christian churches possessed pieces of the sacred 'True Cross' on which Christ was crucified and on which solemn oaths were taken. It is more likely, however, to be much older than this and actually a relic of the prehistoric worship of tree gods, when wood was believed to be the dwelling place of ancient deities and their assistance or protection was sought by touching or knocking on the tree. As a matter of note, the wood should only be touched with the right hand.

Since the dawn of time man has regarded the skies as the dwelling place of the gods, and naturally worship of the heavens and its inhabitants has featured in almost every religion. This explains the origin of the second popular superstition, that good luck can be obtained by making a wish as soon as you see the first evening star in the heavens. You must also repeat these lines:

Star light, Star bright,
First star I see tonight.
I wish I may, I wish I might,
Have the wish I wish tonight.

The reason for the four-leafed clover featuring so highly in the popularity list is not so easy to explain, although the fact that anything unusual tends to excite man's curiosity might have something to do with it. Legend claims that it was the only thing Eve was able to bring with her when she was expelled from Paradise. The often-heard expression that somebody doing well in life is 'in clover' almost certainly stems from the old and well-established fact that cattle graze best and grow fattest when feeding in fields of clover.

The black cat has been one of the most famous creatures in superstition for many centuries. Its traditional association with witchcraft has much to do with this

The horseshoe as a harbinger of good luck has become a commonplace decoration on homes all over the world and those which have been found in the road are supposed to be the luckiest. It must, of course, be hung with the points *upwards* or else the luck will 'run out'. It has been suggested it earned its status because it is made in the form of a 'C' symbolizing Christ, but again it was held in awe long before Christianity developed and could have been seen as a representation of the heavens. As something that was forged from the sacred metal iron in the holy flame of fire, it was regarded in earlier days as doubly endowed, and when it had finished its useful life on a horse's hoof could still be used as a guard against evil and a promoter of fortune.

A black cat crossing your path heads the list as the world's most famous bad luck symbol, although by one of the most striking inconsistencies to be found in the annals of superstition, the reverse is said to be true in the British Isles! The reason for the dislike of the black cat (and it only applies as long as the creature does not have a single white hair on its body) is because its colour is reminiscent of night and the powers of darkness: a sinister-looking, nocturnal animal by nature, it has been considered a consort of evil spirits – in particular witches – since the very earliest times. The reverence with which cats in general are held stems back to the Egyptians who worshipped them as divinities and to the Romans who believed them to be sacred to the goddess Diana.

Breaking a mirror follows the black cat in the catalogue of bad luck. Seven years' misfortune is the penalty for such an accident; the reason lying in the very old idea that a person's reflection is their soul and to smash the mirror results in the damaging of the soul, dooming the person to an early death and depriving them of entry to heaven. There are antidotes to the bad luck, however: in Europe all the pieces of broken glass must be collected up and thrown into a fast flowing stream or river to 'wash away' the bad luck, while in America you should quickly put a five dollar note on the glass splinters and make the sign of the cross. Two death omens associated with the mirror are that if one falls from the wall for no apparent reason or suddenly shatters, then a member of the household is shortly going to die. The same is also true of a framed photograph or portrait.

Numbers feature strongly in our story as subsequent chapters will show, and indeed the subject is so immense that it has its own science, numerology. Of all numbers thirteen is by far the best known, and the most ill-omened; indeed those who fear its influence are said to suffer from 'triskaidekaphobia'. Some authorities think it earned its bad luck because thirteen people sat

The horror at finding thirteen seated for dinner – an engraving by William McConnell (1851)

down to the Last Supper, and with this in mind few hostesses would consider seating thirteen for dinner; there is also a Norse legend that twelve gods gathered for a feast when a thirteenth, Loki, entered, and trouble arose which ended in the death of Balder, the most beloved of the gods. The number thirteen is avoided in all manner of places and situations, with the double association of Friday the thirteenth of any month being particularly ill-omened. More prosaically, H.G. Wells suggested that the thirteen superstition is due to the fact that man was fascinated by the easy and facile manner in which twelve can be split up – three times four, twice six and so on: thirteen cannot be divided at all, he pointed out, and for this reason obtained a bad name.

Two other important numbers to be mentioned here are three and seven. Three features very widely in our lives: think of the number of rituals required to be performed three times such as

Marilyn Monroe in the film
The Seven Year Itch (1954),
inspired by an old
superstition. The ill-fated
Marilyn was herself a very
superstitious person

'three cheers', three spoonfuls of medicine and three demands for a bill to be paid! – while the widespread idea that it is unlucky to light three cigarettes from a single match is relatively a modern superstition, said to have developed during the Boer War when soldiers lighting three cigarettes gave a sniper just enough time to take aim at them and then shoot the man getting the third light. The number seven earned its special importance because it marks the number of days it took God to create the world, and any association with it is said to be lucky. The seventh son of a seventh son is the most fortunate of men, and that popular phrase about the 'seven year itch' is said to have derived from a very old idea that every seven years a man or woman's personality undergoes a complete change.

The fourth and final bad luck superstition is the avoidance of walking underneath a ladder, and there are two explanations as to how this became ill-omened. The first suggests that when a ladder is placed against a wall it forms a natural triangle which is also the symbol of the Holy Trinity, and therefore to walk through it shows a lack of respect and even an association with the Devil. The other explanation for its bad luck is associated with the old type of

Superstition in action –
rather than walk under a
ladder this young lady
squeezes awkwardly around
it!

gallows, where it was propped up against a supporting beam to enable the man about to be hanged to climb up to reach the rope. Whichever might be true, there is no disputing the strength of the superstition and it is common to see people step out into a busy road rather than keep on the pavement and go beneath a ladder. (It is on record that in 1960 members of a psychology class at Bishop Otter College in Chichester set up a ladder in a busy high street and observed what pedestrians did: over 70 per cent preferred to risk stepping into the traffic rather than the bad luck of going under the ladder!) By the way, should you inadvertently walk under one, you can avoid the bad luck by quickly crossing your fingers and keeping them crossed until you see a dog, though why a dog should be able to lift the influence I cannot determine!

These, then, are the most popular good and bad luck superstitions, and the pages which follow record and explain a representative selection of some of the other beliefs to be found around the world. It is doubtful whether it will ever be possible to contain every single superstition and its variations in one volume – indeed

One possible origin of the bad luck superstition associated with walking under a ladder: its old use at the gallows in hanging people

Members of the London
'Thirteen Club' meet to defy
superstition by walking
under ladders and raising
umbrellas indoors. So far
their luck has been good . . .

it has been estimated there must be in excess of 500,000 of them
worldwide – but I believe that at the end the reader will be in no
doubt just how deeply all these beliefs are woven into the fabric of
our societies and lives. And how right Professors McKellar and
Tills are about their impact and influence on us.

Of course there are plenty of people who deliberately set out to
try and debunk superstitions, like, for instance, the members of the
London Thirteen Club who walk under ladders, open umbrellas
indoors, smash mirrors and dine thirteen to a table; all with
seeming impunity. In America there is the National Society of
Thirteen against Superstition, Prejudice and Fear which meets on
Friday the thirteenth, and whose members similarly try to go
contrary to any old belief and have yet to suffer any repercussions
for their effrontery. It is a fact, though, that whether the attempts
at debunking are humorous or serious, undertaken by practical
joker or respected scholar, the hold of superstition has not been
weakened a jot. And, as one American professor of folklore pointed
out to me, what chance have they got when even the most modern
advances in science somehow fall under its influence?

Superstition and space flight – the American rocket *Vanguard III* carried a St Christopher medallion to ward off misfortune

He was referring to the great achievement of spaceflight. The space rocket Vanguard III, he told me, carried a Saint Christopher medallion, the ancient symbol of protection for travellers, while several of the astronauts insisted on the ill-omened colours of yellow and green being avoided on any item of equipment. But such things passed into insignificance when the mission of Apollo 13 was launched on 11 April 1970, for two days later, on the fateful *thirteenth*, the explosion of an oxygen tank aborted the moon mission and nearly cost the lives of the three astronauts. From mankind's dark past superstition seemed to have reached out yet again to touch the affairs of men . . .

Symbol of the ill-fated American space mission, *Apollo 13*, which turned into a disaster on 13 April 1970

CHAPTER 2

SUPERSTITION AND YOU

The story of Adam and Eve
can be traced as the root of
many of our present day
superstitions. A fine
engraving by Gustave Doré

SUPERSTITION AND YOU

Superstition says that a hairy chest like that of Tony Curtis' is a sure sign of masculinity. Tony is himself a very superstitious person with a particular fear of white cats crossing his path!

Queen Elizabeth I, a red-head who lived up to the belief that all such people are fiery-tempered. An engraving of the Queen knighting Sir Francis Drake.

Some of man's most enduring and unchanging superstitions concern himself and his own body, and as a group they are particularly interesting because they underline the age-old concern with health and longevity. From the very earliest times man has naturally enough sought every possible aid to protect himself from the evil influence which threatened his existence on all sides, and predictably there is a noticeable searching for good signs rather than bad ones wherever one looks. The complexity and multiplicity of superstitions concerning the human body are such that it is only possible to consider the more widespread of the beliefs, and in an attempt to impose some sort of order over this discussion it is well to start at the head and move down the body from there.

The hair, 'the crowning glory' as it is so often described in the case of a woman, is known to be one of the most indestructible parts of the body, and therefore any sudden loss of hair is bound to be unlucky. According to traditions found all over the world, such a loss forecasts a decline in health, loss of property or failure in business, or even the death of a closely related child.

Types of hair are also important: red hair has always been associated with fiery-tempered people – Cleopatra and Queen Elizabeth I are two famous examples – while black and dark brown hair indicate strength, and fair hair the timid. It has been said that

Another fiery red-head,
Queen Cleopatra, from a
nineteenth-century
biography of her life

the reason for the prejudice against red hair is that it was the colour of Judas Iscariot's hair. The way hair grows can also be an omen: on a man, if the hair grows low on the forehead and back above the temples he will have a long life; while if a woman's hair grows in a low point on her forehead then this 'widow's peak' means she will outlive her husband. Any lady whose hair suddenly develops curls on the forehead should also beware: it is a sign her man has not long to live. Lank hair has always been seen as indicating a cunning nature, but the curly-headed are good natured and full of fun. Long hair is supposed to indicate strength (*vide* Samson) and be lucky – as the Beatles pop group found when they changed their hairstyles and became world-famous.

Although most women will probably not have the time to check the fact, it is said to be unlucky to have your hair cut when the moon is on the wane as this will cause it to fall and lose its lustre. It is also tempting fate to cut your own hair: but you may use some strands to determine your future. If you set fire to these and they burn brightly, you are in for a long life; should they splutter and smoulder, it is said in many parts of the world to be a death omen. On a lighter note, never pull out grey hairs: superstition says each one will be replaced by ten more; and though the old tradition that sudden fright can turn the hair white is often scoffed at, history is replete with cases where just that happened.

The colour of people's eyes, women's in particular, has been a source of admiration for poets and writers for centuries, yet the beliefs about this are rooted in superstition. Tradition says that those with dark blue eyes are delicate and refined souls, while those with light blue and grey eyes are strong and healthy. Green eyes are also a sign of the hardy, while those with hazel eyes are vigorous, deep-thinking folk. In parts of America I found that it was believed black-eyed girls were deceitful and those with grey eyes, greedy.

Throughout the world itching eyes are believed to be omens: if it is the right eye that tickles then you are about to be lucky, the other way round – watch out! From the earliest times a lover with an itching right eye might soon expect a reunion with his beloved; Theocritus wrote: 'My right eye itches now and I shall see my love.' Another European rhyme warns us against those whose eyebrows meet across the nose:

Trust not the man whose eyebrows meet,
For in his heart you'll find deceit.

Perhaps even more intriguing is the middle-European superstition which I have heard repeated more than once, that such a person is likely to be a werewolf!

Superstition maintains that the eyes reveal the character of a person. Bela Lugosi, who was the first great screen Dracula in the 1930s, believed in many superstitions and carried several good luck charms – though none to ward off vampires!

By no means so chilling, yet still ominous, was the superstition I learnt in America that a prominent vein across the bridge of the nose was a sign of an early death; on this side of the Atlantic, I was told, the vein was just a sign that the person would never marry.

Tingling ears also feature prominently in superstition, and an old Scottish relative of mine used to repeat whenever anyone scratched their ear: 'Right lug, left lug, whilk lug lows. If the left ear they talk harm, if the right ear, good.' According to the tradition, ears tickle when someone is talking about you, and it is your guardian angel who tickles you to indicate if you are being spoken well of or ill; if it is the left ear that proves troublesome, it is said in some European countries you can put a stop to whoever is speaking badly of you by biting your tongue; exactly the same thing will then apparently happen to the ill-wisher.

Phrenologists have of late been busy 'proving' that small ears denote a delicate character and thick ears a person of a sensual and coarse nature. Superstition has been saying this for centuries, adding that thin, angular ears denote a bad temper, and long or prominent ears a person with musical inclinations. The larger the ear lobes, too, the greater the intellect. Burning cheeks are often spoken of in the same context as tingling ears, and said to indicate that someone is speaking good or ill of you whether the right side or left, but here there is usually a rational explanation in that you are undergoing some kind of emotional stress at the moment in question to cause the blush.

Superstition has had plenty to say about the nose over the years, and those two great soldiers Wellington and Napoleon both believed its shape indicated the character of the man. Prominent noses are said to indicate intelligence and determination; thin

An example of superstition showing the characteristics of a thick-witted person (left) and a brutal, over-bearing person. From *Physiogno-monia*, written by Barthélemy Coclès in the sixteenth century

The Duke of Wellington believed in the superstition that it was possible to tell the character of a man by his nose. He was certainly the possessor of a fine example!

noses jealousy and uncertainty; receding noses bad temper and obstinacy; tip-tilted noses bright and lively characters. For many centuries it has been said there is a direct relationship between the size of a person's nose and their sexual organs. A tickling nose in Britain is said to foretell a fight or an important communication, while in America you can expect a kiss.

Shakespeare is one of many writers who have noted that a nose bleed is a bad-omen, although just one drop of blood is a sign of good fortune to come. For a boy or girl to have a nose bleed in the presence of their lover is a particularly good sign, for they are surely in love. The many old cures for supposedly stopping a nose bleed really have no place here, but it is worth noting that the old expression 'paying through the nose' for something actually originated in Sweden, where a tax was once levied on the basis of a charge being made for each nose of the population counted.

A pleasant superstition holds that itching or tingling lips are a sign that someone is soon going to kiss you and I have heard this tradition repeated as widely as the claim that if you bite your tongue while you are eating then the reason for this is that you have very recently told a lie. As someone with a large gap between my two front teeth, I have been unable to dismiss the idea that I shall be lucky in life. Large teeth are claimed to indicate physical strength, while those with small, regular teeth will always be careful and methodical in their habits. There are not many bad omens attached to teeth, except that it is not a good sign for a child to be born with any teeth showing, and if the first tooth to appear is in an infant's upper jaw then it is doomed to die young.

There are many old fashioned remedies for supposedly curing toothache, but in this day and age there is no better advice than suggesting a visit to the dentist. In America I was warned never to eat anything when a funeral bell was tolling as toothache would surely result.

It is perhaps not surprising that the hand, used in almost every activity, should be surrounded by superstitions, and there are many good luck tokens and charms shaped like a hand. It has always been regarded as symbolic of power and it is also used as an instrument of healing, justice and blessing. The right hand is considered lucky, and the left unlucky because the Devil was said to have sat on the left-hand side of God before being cast out of heaven.

The kings of England from the time of Edward the Confessor are said to have had the power to 'heal by touch', a belief that no doubt developed from the ancient idea that people of the very highest rank possessed special powers denied to ordinary mortals. By

Superstition has long maintained that anyone whose eyebrows meet across the bridge of their nose can become a werewolf! Lon Chaney played the famous 'wolf man' in a series of films made by Universal Pictures in the 1940s

Robbers using a 'Hand of Glory' to open a locked door. An illustration of this old superstition by Paul Hardy from *Half-Hours with the Highwaymen* by Charles G. Harper (1908)

contrast, the hand of an executed criminal, cut from his body while still on the gallows, was said to have healing powers as well as providing its owners with the ability to commit crime and robbery without fear of detection by stupefying all those who saw it. There are indeed many gruesome stories of the use of these 'Hands of Glory'; here is one from *The Irish Times* of 13 January 1831. A group of thieves had attempted to commit a robbery on the estate of a Mr Napier of Loughscrew in County Meath. The report states:

The men entered the house armed with a dead man's hand with a lighted candle in it, believing in the superstitious notion that a candle placed in a dead man's hand will not be seen and will prevent those who may be asleep from awaking. The inmates, however, were alarmed and the robbers fled leaving the hand behind them.

Superstition tells us that large, thick hands denote strength of character, while small slender hands are found on the weak and timid. Long hands reveal an ingenious nature, while short ones are said to be found on people who are careless and foolish. Hard hands indicate rudeness, soft ones wit, and those covered with hair a person who likes luxury.

If the palm of your right hand starts to itch it is a sign that you will shortly be receiving some money, but if it is the left one which troubles you then you are going to lose some, or more than likely pay out some big bills. (In America I was told you can break this possibility by rubbing your hand quickly on a piece of wood.) It has always been bad luck to shake hands with the left hand, and there can hardly be a reader who has not heard the old saying that a damp hand is the sign of an amorous disposition while 'a cold hand means a warm heart'. Country friends have told me two people should never wash their hands together in the same water as this will lead to a quarrel between them.

Fingers have almost as many superstitions about them as the hand, and the idea of crossing the first and second fingers – in effect making the sign of the cross with its protective powers – to ward off bad luck is universal in application. Children with long fingers are said to be destined to follow artistic pursuits, while those with short and thick fingers will probably be intemperate and silly. A crooked little finger has long been seen as an omen of wealth, while the first forefinger is traditionally known as the 'poison finger' and should never be used for applying any medicines. The third finger on the left hand was in the earliest times erroneously believed to be the luckiest of all because it was linked directly to the heart: this is the reason why it was chosen as the finger on which the wedding ring should be worn.

SUPERSTITION AND YOU

A Roman bronze hand embellished with luck-bringing powers. From the British Museum

Many Kings of England have been credited with having a healing power in their touch. Charles I is seen here laying hands on sufferers from scrofula in 1629: an illustration from an old broadsheet

The reason for finger nails featuring in superstition is primarily because the clippings were believed to be one of the essential ingredients used by a witch putting a spell on someone. It is unlucky to cut them on Friday or Sunday, and in many places it is said that the size of the 'half moon' shape at the base indicates by its size whether the person will have a long life or short. The spots sometimes found on nails are also ominous, Robert Burton says in his *Anatomy of Melancholy* (1621): yellow specks indicate death, black spots ill-luck, while white spots are a sign of good fortune to come.

In England I have heard it said that any woman who can cut the nails of her right hand with her left will have the upper hand in marriage, and in America there is a tradition that the same will apply if the woman has a big toe which is shorter in length than the second one. On the subject of feet, an itching foot is supposed to indicate that you will shortly go on a journey to somewhere new, while all flat-footed people are supposed to be bad-tempered; it is further said to be unlucky to enter any buildings with your left foot first.

Having covered the body from head to toe, let us now consider those little body markings, the moles and dimples, that in the past attracted such attention among the superstitious that whole books were devoted to the many interpretations put on their appearance and position on the body. Moles on the lefthand side of the body are said to be unlucky, those on the right lucky; on the face, particularly on the chin or neck, they are said to indicate wealth, while on the chest and stomach, strength. (Incidentally, a hairy chest is supposed to be a sign of masculinity.) A mole on the nose is said to be a sign of great lechery, while a mole on a woman's thigh reveals she will be unfaithful and a great spendthrift; however, the girl fortunate enough to have one on her breast will be irresistible.

SUPERSTITION AND YOU

The dimple has a different interpretation depending on which side of the Atlantic you live. In Britain they are believed to be lucky because they were made by the impression of God's finger; but in America they are ill-omened, having been made by the Evil One as this rhyme says: 'Dimple on the chin – Devil within.' Superstition also maintains the wart was produced by the Devil's touch, and is similarly unlucky; even to list the multitude of supposed cures for this blemish would surely fill all our remaining space.

Tradition has also been busy with all those little complaints that effect us from day to day – sneezes, coughs, yawns, shivers, and so on. The act of sneezing – a 'little death' as it is called in certain places where it is believed the soul momentarily leaves the body – has been the subject of superstition since the very earliest times. At first it was considered a good omen to sneeze (Aristotle notes that his contemporaries considered it divine), and it was customary to salute anyone doing so. It took on a more sinister implication during the Roman era, when it was noticed that sneezing could sometimes be the first indication that a person had caught the plague, and the custom developed of people reciting the words 'God bless you' to anyone who sneezed, in case they had caught the plague and would soon be dead or confined in isolation. Today we still use the expression shorn of its first word when someone sneezes, probably quite unaware of its origin.

Children have their own saying about the implications of sneezing more than once: 'Once a wish, twice a kiss, three times something better' (alternatively 'a letter'). And in Scotland it is still said that a newborn child remains under 'the fairy spells' until it has sneezed for the first time. Elsewhere similar importance is placed on a child's first sneeze because of the erroneous belief that no idiot could ever sneeze. Among the more lighthearted beliefs about sneezing, it is said in America that if you sneeze while talking it is a sign you are telling the truth, in Germany three sneezes before breakfast means you will receive a present during the day, while the Japanese believe that any sneeze is an indication that somebody, somewhere, is saying nice things about you. The best piece of luck attached to sneezing is if you should sneeze at exactly the same time as someone else you are with.

A sudden bout of coughing was attributed by superstition to the unexpected entry of a devil into a person who had been telling lies or carrying out misdemeanours of some kind. It is perhaps as well that this idea seems to have died out in most places, as one of the most popular remedies for a cough was a drink made of barley water in which three snails had been boiled! Throughout Europe you can still hear the belief that hiccoughs are caused by someone

Engraving from a
seventeenth-century treatise
on the omens to be drawn
from the positions of moles
on a person's face

41

Sir Walter Scott, who was largely responsible for giving the opal its unlucky reputation in his novel *Anne of Geierstein* (1831)

who dislikes you complaining about you to someone else. Apparently the only way to put a stop to this is to guess the name of the person maligning you.

Superstition is also at the back of the habit of covering the mouth with the hand when yawning for it was once believed that evil spirits used the opportunity of a yawn to enter the body unless the mouth was covered. In America the Indians also have a tradition that a yawn is a sign Death is calling to you, and to avoid this fate you should snap your second finger and thumb.

An involuntary shiver has for generations been believed to be a sign someone is walking over the spot where you will eventually be buried. A palpitation of any of the muscles is a good sign if it happens on the right side of the body, but a bad one on the left, which doubtless has much to do with the fact that the heart is located on the left hand side. The sensation of a 'ringing in the ears' is, according to one tradition, an omen that death is not far away – although it is not necessarily going to strike either the person concerned or those close to him. Throughout Europe, though, this sound is taken to mean that someone is talking about you: if the sound is in your right ear it is your husband or wife (or lover), if in the left then it is your mother.

And so to laughter, of which I have heard country folk say that to laugh before breakfast will result in tears before supper. In some countries, too, it is believed that to laugh excessively is a bad sign, for the person gives all the appearance of being 'possessed' by his laughter and therefore his days are numbered.

Jewellery features strongly in superstition, primarily because such adornments were first put on the body to protect it from evil spirits. Man once believed that these spirits were forever trying to enter the body by one or other of the five orifices, and decorating them was the best way to prevent such entry. Earrings were particularly important as talismans to keep devils out of the ears, and the painting of lips served the same purpose. So far as specific jewels are concerned, emeralds got their unlucky reputation because they were much used in the East for the eyes of religious figures and consequently became the target of robbers. The opal was labelled 'the patron of thieves' by Albertus Magnus, a thirteenth-century alchemist – he maintained that an opal wrapped in bay leaves made its wearer invisible. Opals are certainly considered unlucky today. In literature they tend to feature in rather sinister roles, notably in Sir Walter Scott's novel, *Anne of Geierstein* (1831), in which a character disappears after holy water falls on the opal in her hair. Pearls have changed their aura: they were once believed to be unlucky – people in Medieval times

42

thought they were 'solidified tears' — whereas nowadays many owners claim that the gift of a string of pearls has brought them great good luck! Diamonds are the best of all good luck bringers, hence their use in so many rings, and superstition says they also possess the power to drive off witches and prevent the wearer from ever going insane.

The clothes we wear are just as subject to superstition as our bodies, and over the years a substantial number of beliefs have evolved. It is probably true to say that clothing superstitions are simply extensions of the older traditions associated with the human body, and that many of them developed their special properties because of their relationship with parts of the body held to have magical virtues. For example, the glove which covers the hand, so highly revered in superstition: it is unlucky to drop your glove and pick it up yourself, whereas if someone else does it, there is good fortune in store for both of you.

The young actress Diana Dors with a string of lucky pearls. These stones were once believed to be solidified tears

SUPERSTITION AND YOU

William I, who originated the belief that it is lucky to inadvertently put on an item of clothing inside out

The most famous of clothing superstitions is the belief that it is lucky to put on an item of clothing accidentally inside out, although you must not change it until the time you would normally take it off for the luck to hold. This belief originated with William of Normandy who inadvertently put on his shirt of mail back to front just before the Battle of Hastings; when his courtiers pointed out his mistake and said it was a bad omen, quick-thinking William assured them it was not and was in fact a sign he was about to be changed from a duke into a king. From such a simple beginning was one of our commonest superstitions born.

It has always been unlucky to hook or button up any item of clothing wrongly (start all over again if you do), just as you should never put your left arm, leg or foot into anything first. (Our old friend the Devil will take advantage of this lapse if you do!) No doubt because it is closest to the body, underwear has attracted a cluster of beliefs. If a girl's bra or pants should suddenly slip down (and I am assured the same applies to stockings) then this is a sign that someone who loves her is thinking of her; while if two or more holes should appear in any of these items then tradition says the owner can expect a gift very shortly. Any girl wearing suspenders who finds that her stocking slips from the clasp three times can take it she is in for an unlucky day, but if stockings or tights left to dry

Right: A turn of the century sketch of some of the lucky items of underwear a girl could wear – from *La Vie Parisienne*, 1908

Left: The American actress Jane Russell had good cause to believe in the luck of underwear – it was a specially designed brassiere which shot her to international stardom in the film *The Outlaw*

on the washing line curl up around each other it is an omen that the owner may expect great happiness before long. Garters have always been regarded as lucky, and many a girl has slept with one under her pillow on Midsummer Eve in the hope of dreaming of her future husband (a suspender belt can also do the trick, apparently). Superstition likewise instructs any young girl anxious for a husband to get a garter recently worn by a married woman and put it on her own leg; she will not then have to wait long for Mr Right to turn up. Welsh country lore also says a girl who puts valerian in her underwear will prove irresistible to men.

The growing modern practice among young girls of not wearing underwear – bras in particular – has an interesting parallel in superstition: it used to be considered very lucky for a bride to get

Superstition says that a girl who puts on a man's hat is inviting him to kiss her! A still from the film of Harold Robbins' novel *The Carpetbaggers*

The ancient superstition against wearing green clothes reappears in a modern setting. From *The Times*, 22 October 1977

Job lost for refusal to wear green

A woman said to have a deep-seated superstition against wearing green lost her job in a canteen after she refused to wear a new green and white uniform.

A London industrial tribunal yesterday dismissed with regret a claim by Mrs Kathleen Roberts, of Chessington, Surrey, that she had been unfairly dismissed by the Sutcliffe Catering Company (South) Ltd, after eight years' employment in the Borax company's canteen in Cox Lane, Chessington.

Mr Eric Wrintmore, chairman, said the employers fully recognized the quality of her work. They proposed to change the uniform colour scheme next year and had given an assurance that if there should be a vacancy at that time she would be welcomed back.

Mrs Roberts was dismissed in May with eight weeks' salary in lieu of notice, after being warned for refusing to wear the uniform.

Mr Wrintmore said that Sutcliffe Catering was not unreasonable in wanting to implement "a uniform policy and to implement that policy uniformly".

married with nothing on under her wedding gown. The origin of this tradition was that until well into the nineteenth century a new husband became liable for any debts previously incurred by his bride; but, it was believed, if the girl went to the altar wearing no more than her dress, any creditors would take pity on such an obviously poor young soul and not wish to compound the problems in her new life by pressing their bills. Such ceremonies were known as 'smock' weddings.

The association of clothes with body magic seems to have reached a high point in this era of superstars in the worlds of entertainment and sport as is evidenced by young fans wanting to touch their idols and, where possible, actually grab pieces of their clothing, believing such items will somehow bring them good luck. Strangely, it is also a good luck sign if either a man or woman accidentally burns or singes any item of their clothing while visiting friends: superstition says this is a sure sign they will visit again. Some American friends told me that to find the hem of any garment turned up is an omen that you will be getting a similar brand new item before long. By way of contrast, some Essex folk told me that it is unlucky to wear clothes that have belonged to anyone who has died, for as the body of the deceased decays so will the clothes; these people have a saying which runs, 'The clothes of the dead always wear full of holes'.

The humble handkerchief features in another interesting superstition. The idea of tying a knot in it to remind yourself of something actually evolved from a very ancient belief that the knot was a charm against evil, for should any demon be nearby when you tie the knot he will be so intrigued by the shape you have created that all thoughts of interfering with you will go from his mind. Hats, too, have their own tradition that a bad day will result from putting one on back to front, and in America it is said that a woman who puts on a man's hat is giving a sign she wants to be kissed.

The shoe is another luck-bringer, hence the custom of tying an old boot to the back of the car of a couple who have just got married; but only misfortune will dog anyone foolish enough to put a pair of shoes on a table, for this is said to be symbolic of hanging. Shoes should never be left crossed on the floor, you should avoid putting shoes on the wrong feet, and it is challenging fate to walk anywhere with only one shoe on as it could lead to the death of one or other of your parents. If a shoelace comes undone as you are setting off on some venture it is a bad sign, but it is lucky to tie someone else's shoe laces up and you should make a wish as you do so. Personally, my favourite shoe superstition has been the old

country belief that if a new pair of shoes squeak a lot it is a sign the owner has not yet paid for them!

Lastly, some general words of advice about clothes. When you first put on a new suit or dress always slip a small coin into the right-hand pocket: or you will always be hard up when you wear that particular item. (A coin should similarly be put into a new purse or handbag to ensure it thereafter always has a supply of money.) Never mend any item of clothing while wearing it. And it is always good luck to wear some new item of clothing on Easter Day – a continuation of the old tradition that everything old and dirty should be renewed at the festival of Eastertide. I hope husbands will forgive me for adding that in America it is stated a woman can only look forward to good fortune and happiness in Spring if she wears *three* new things on Easter Sunday!

Left: The old custom of throwing slippers at newly-weds illustrated in an engraving from *The Illustrated London News* of the marriage of Princess Louise in 1871

Right: The Easter bunny makes an appearance during an Easter Sunday parade in New York

CHAPTER 3

BELIEFS OF
THE HOME

Oakley Court, a strange
Victorian-Gothic mansion at
Bray in Berkshire, which is
said to have an 'evil
atmosphere'. It has several
times been used as the
location for the making of
horror films

BELIEFS OF THE HOME

There is a strong and continuing belief, which I admit to sharing myself, that all houses have either a warm and friendly atmosphere or one that is cold and depressing. It makes no difference whether the house is new or has stood for centuries, nor for that matter what kind of heating or insulation there is; if the place has an inherently hostile atmosphere nothing can change this to a friendly one. This is known as the 'spirit of the house' and it dates from earlier times when the home was literally believed to be under the auspices of a spirit whose personality governed whether the place enjoyed good or bad luck.

Because so much of human life goes on within the home, it has taken on a special place in superstition and consciously or unconsciously many of the things we do within its four walls are influenced by customs which are of great antiquity and almost impossible to explain today. For example, superstition is at the bottom of the tradition of taking gifts to those who have just moved into a new home. The gifts should in fact be for the house rather than the people, for when the idea first evolved the presents were supposed to be for the 'spirit of the house' as a form of propitiation. In very early times, too, it was common for a living creature to be buried in the walls of a house or building as it was being erected as an actual sacrifice to these spirits. (Subconsciously, we continue this tradition by burying small containers of items like newspapers, coins, and other accoutrements of modern living, in the foundations of important new constructions.)

Superstition at work – the windows of an old house in Essex left open while an elderly man inside is dying, thereby allowing his soul an easy passage to heaven

The kitchen and the act of cooking has been surrounded by omens and superstitions since the very earliest times. One of the oldest beliefs is that any food stirred anti-clockwise will never taste right

The door, as the main point of entry into the house, has always had a place of particular importance in superstition, and the positioning over the porch of statues and good luck symbols (such as the famous horseshoe which must, of course, have the points upwards) has been specifically to keep out bad elements either human or spiritual. It has always been considered unlucky to enter a new home for the first time by the back door, as this entrance is not protected against evil spirits and they will take this opportunity to slip into the place. Visitors, incidentally, should always be encouraged to leave the house by the same door they entered or else they will take the owner's luck with them, according to American superstition. The opening of a door by its own accord is an omen that a visitor is on the way, probably an unwelcome one for some reason; while a door that slams is also a bad sign for should the 'spirit of the house' be passing at that time and be hit or even trapped, his attitude towards the household might very well change. In any event, whoever was responsible for slamming the door is in for a bad day.

Although it is unlucky, as well as foolhardy, to leave all the doors and windows of a home open when no one is there (evil spirits as well as burglars could slip in), superstition does say that they should be open when a child is being born or someone is dying so that the entry or exit may take place without hindrance. The Romans particularly observed this custom, and they even feared that anyone who entered a home with his left foot first might bring in bad luck; so a servant was always on duty at the door to prevent this happening, these men being the forerunners of the modern footman.

The home is, of course, very much under the control of the housewife and the heart of her domain is certainly the kitchen where superstition has found a much greater sway over activities than might at first be expected. There can hardly be a cook anywhere who does not follow the maxim that when any food is mixed it should be stirred clockwise. Perhaps unconsciously she is following the old idea that anything stirred anti-clockwise would never taste right, but what she *is* doing is paying deference to one of the oldest beliefs connected with sun-worship, that all functions of importance should be performed in an east to west direction. And just how automatically does a cook always leave a tray or cooking utensil of some kind in the oven even when it is not in use? This action has its roots in the old Jewish superstition that an oven which is left completely empty is tempting the fates, for the time may come when the owner has nothing to place in it.

The conscientious housewife also never wastes the pieces of pastry or dough left over from making cakes or bread, but turns them into small morsels for the children. Again the origins of this custom hark back to superstition and the belief that if any scraps were left over the whole baking would be ruined unless they were given to a child to eat up.

Although not as many women make their own bread as used to – though the practice does seem to be coming back into favour – it is still known in many places as the 'staff of life'. The habit of marking loaves with a cross to protect them from evil is still in evidence, and an old countryman told me that a wadge of such bread pressed against an aching tooth would relieve the pain. When baking bread, a wife would be well advised to remember the lines:

> She that pricks bread with fork or knife
> Will never be a happy maid or wife.

A loaf that splits open while it is in the oven is said to be a warning of death to come in the family, and a loaf that proves to have a hollow centre also presages death. It is unlucky to turn a loaf upside down after cutting the first slice for this will cause the head of the household to fall ill; and if a loaf crumbles in your hand as you are cutting it there is going to be a quarrel before very long. You might like to note, too, that if you drop a slice of buttered bread and the butter side faces up, then an old belief says a visitor is imminent.

There is an omen to be found in cooking a joint of meat: according to a story repeated all over Europe, if the joint shrinks then misfortune is on the way to the family, while if it swells the sign indicates a prosperous future.

Superstition says that all scraps of dough and pastry must be used up or the whole baking will be ruined

Witches have the ability to put spells on food, according to superstition, and will often use ordinary ingredients for their magic

The egg is another important item of food surrounded by superstition. It is a very common practice for someone who has finished a boiled egg to either crush the shell or push their spoon through the bottom so as to avoid bad luck. Most of those who do this are probably unaware that they are performing an age-old ritual which stems from the belief that witches collected up empty egg shells and used them to go to sea and work their spells against hapless mariners. Country people believe it is bad luck to bring eggs into the house after dark (whether they have been collected or bought from a shop), and any double-yoked egg used to be considered in parts of Britain as an omen of death to come in the owner's family. The particular regard in which the egg is held dates from antiquity when the Egyptians and Romans among others saw its shape as an emblem of the Universe and consequently the work of the greatest

The egg has been held in high regard since the very earliest times as a symbol of the universe, and consequently is the object of several superstitions

After salt has been spilled a pinch of it should be thrown over the left shoulder to avoid bad luck. Here a member of the Thirteen Club defies the old superstition by deliberately spilling some

of the gods. The giving of Easter eggs and the use of eggs in all sorts of other festivities, both Christian and those held by other religions, can be traced back to this very early veneration.

Perhaps no superstition from the kitchen is more firmly imprinted on our consciousness than the bad luck attached to spilling salt. We all know that to counter this a pinch must be taken and thrown over the left shoulder – but why? It seems that the Ancient Greeks played a major part in shaping this tradition for they believed that salt was sacred and a repository of life itself because of its powers as a preservative, and consequently used it in their sacrificial cakes and preparations. They also believed it was a symbol of friendship, and therefore if any was spilled it was an omen of the end of a friendship. (Among some peoples it was the custom to pay workers in amounts of salt, hence our modern word salary, from *salarium*.) The countering of the charm by throwing salt over the shoulder may be of a later origin and came about because evil spirits – the Devil in particular – were supposed to dwell on the left-hand side of the body, and should one be lurking there to take advantage of the misfortune caused by the accident, the salt would go in his eyes and put a stop to such ideas. Because of

The ordinary kitchen knife plays a part in superstition – and it is important when given one as a present to offer a coin in return to avoid 'cutting' the friendship

the regard in which it is held, salt is often given to newborn babies for luck and in the hope that they will want for nothing in life, and country folk in both Britain and Europe are known to carry little bags of salt on their person to bring them luck in all their dealings. In America I have heard it claimed that for every grain of salt spilt the person concerned will have a day of sorrow, although this can be avoided if the salt is carefully picked up and thrown over the fire, thereby 'drying up' the tears which would be shed.

Tea, that other ever-present in the kitchen, is also the subject of two superstitions. To stir the tea-pot anti-clockwise will stir up a quarrel, while if two women pour from the same pot one of them will have a baby within a year. As to what can be divined from tea-leaves, that topic requires a book of its own.

The ordinary knife has a place in our survey, as for two of them to be found crossed is an ill-omen, and it is interesting to note that the practice of laying knives and forks side by side on the table is a direct result of less peaceful times when a man always held his knife in his hand while eating in case of attack and could only demonstrate friendship to those who shared his table by putting it down. It is also still traditional in some places to give anyone who presents you with a knife a coin in return to avoid 'cutting' the friendship. Superstition has always credited the knife made of iron with the power of protection against witches and evil spirits, and Robert Herrick in one of his verses tells us:

Let the superstitious wife
Near the child's heart lay a knife.
Point be up, and haft be down,
While she gossips in the town.
This amongst other mystic charms
Keeps the sleeping child from harms.

The spoon, too, can be a pointer to the future, for if two are found in a tea cup then there will be a wedding in the family, while if you drop one and it lands with the bowl upwards you are in for a pleasant surprise. Some Scottish relatives also told me that whichever hand a young child uses to reach out for its spoon is an omen for its future; the right hand is an indication of good fortune, while the left is bad.

In Europe there are several instances of superstitions attached to housewives' aprons, and it is said to be lucky accidentally to put one on inside out, but unlucky if it falls off suddenly for no apparent reason. Perhaps the most fascinating of these beliefs is the idea that if a man wipes his hands on a woman's apron he will soon fall in love with her. The explanation for this, I am told, is that as bodily perspiration plays a major part in the attraction of the sexes

– a woman's perspiration is bound to be found on her apron – such contact could well be the first step to falling in love! By contrast, members of the opposite sex should never dry themselves on the same towel as this will invariably lead to a quarrel between them.

Even the task of washing up has attracted its own customs. If you break a plate or cup you can expect another breakage before the end of the day unless you deliberately smash some other small useless item to avoid the bad luck. My male readers will probably not thank me for adding the American verse about washing up which states:

Wash and wipe together
Live in peace together.

An English country superstition says that it is bad luck to throw any water out of the house after nightfall because it has long been regarded as a deterrent to the denizens of the night and by throwing it out you are weakening your protection during the hours of darkness. Don't allow two people to wash in the same water at the same time for this is also said to be ill-omened. As for doing the family wash, the reason for Monday having become the housewife's favourite day seems to be explained in this old English verse:

They that wash on Monday, have the whole week to dry.
They that wash on Tuesday, are not so much awry.
They that wash on Wednesday, will get their clothes so clean.
They that wash on Thursday, are not so much to mean.
They that wash on Friday, wash for their need.
But they that wash on Saturdays are dirty folks indeed.

There are fewer superstitions attached to dining, whether in the kitchen or the dining room, perhaps because from early times eating was considered almost a sacred undertaking and therefore

The famous 'Savoy Black Cat' who is always ready to be brought to a table as a 'guest' when the unlucky number of thirteen people meet for dinner at the famous London hotel

LE MIROIR DU DIABLE

A French illustration of the last century showing how the Devil waits with seven years' bad luck for anyone who breaks a mirror

A George Cruikshank engraving of a man who impertinently poked someone else's fire before he had known them seven years, thereby bringing bad luck upon the family

protected by the gods. You would be as well, though, to look carefully at the tablecloth when the table is being laid, for if a diamond or 'coffin' shape crease is found as it is unfolded this is a death omen. Take care, too, when rising from the table not to upset your chair, for if you do it is a sign that you have lied at some time during your conversation. The Americans in particular have a special regard for the dining-table for they believe that anyone who lies down on a table will die within a year; that any engaged girl who sits on a table while talking to her fiancé risks losing him; and that it is unlucky to change your position after a place has been allocated to you. And it is fairly widely believed that to place your chair back against the wall or fold up your napkin after a meal at a friend's home will prevent you ever visiting there again.

The fireplace has always had a special place in superstition, doubtless because fire was regarded by primitive man as the sacred flame of the gods and something to be regarded with great care. Today it is not uncommon to hear people say that a fire which is difficult to light can be coaxed into life by placing the poker upright against the bars of the grate: this in effect creates a cross shape and is supposed to drive off the evil spirits which are clearly preventing the fire from lighting. These same people also say it is

A superstitious person's nightmare! An illustration of two of the most ill-omened things you can do: stumble on the staircase or pass someone while going up or down

impossible to light a fire in the direct rays of the sun, for fire was originally stolen from the sun and it still prevents any mere flame emulating its power. A fire that roars up the chimney is said to be an omen of an argument or a storm; sparks clinging to the back of the chimney are a sign of important news in the offing; while a sudden fall of soot presages bad weather or a disaster of some kind. Coal, as symbolic of fire, is considered lucky and country people often carry small pieces in their pocket, and of course its use in the tradition of 'first footing' on New Year's Eve is well known.

Mirrors and looking-glasses, which are often found above the fireplace, are subject to a very famous superstition that to break one will result in seven years of bad luck. The origin of this belief can be traced back to early man who, when he saw his image reflected in water, believed it represented his soul and should anything disturb this image then his own life was in danger, hence the shattering of a glass could foreshadow the viewer's own death. Mirrors have always been closely associated with magic, and the great Elizabethan astrologer Dr John Dee used them extensively in his predictions and did much to enhance their position in superstition. It is not uncommon to find mirrors covered over with cloth in the room where someone has died for fear that anyone who sees himself in the glass will similarly die. Napoleon Bonaparte was a firm believer in mirror superstitions and when, during one of his campaigns, he accidentally broke the glass on a portrait of his beloved Josephine he could not sleep until a messenger had been despatched and returned with the news that she was safe and well, and not dead as he feared.

Staircases are subject to just as famous a superstition. It is unlucky to pass anybody on one, and if this is quite unavoidable then you should cross your fingers as you do so. We cannot be sure how this belief originated, but it was either as a result of the ancient conviction that stairways symbolized the means of ascending to the abode of the gods and it was dangerous to trespass, or because early stairways were very narrow and as two people passed each other they left themselves open to attack from behind. On the other hand, stumbling on the stairway is said to be a good omen and can even indicate a wedding in the household before long.

Safely upstairs, we are still not free from misfortune. It is advisable, for instance, not to sing in the bath in the morning for this will lead to sorrow before evening, and any young girl who persistently splashes herself or her clothes when she is washing had better watch out for she will end up with a husband who is a drunk. Of course getting a good start to the day is of the utmost importance and has given rise to the expression about getting out of bed

The bedroom has attracted more than its fair share of superstitions – and everyone should beware of getting out of the bed on the wrong side!

the right side. The left-hand side has always been considered the 'wrong' side because of its association with the Devil, but if you have no alternative but to get out this side, you can counteract the bad luck by putting your right sock and shoe on first. It is said you will always get the best sleep if your bed is positioned in a north–south direction, with your head to the south, as this will ensure a long life. If you want the chance to be rich, point the head towards the east, but if travel is your objective head it to the west. (Interestingly several doctors have said that a good night's rest *does* seem to be more easily obtained in a bed pointing south, though they can think of no logical reason why this should be so!) In America it is claimed to be unlucky to put a hat down on a bed, and in parts of England there are still those who would not dream of going to bed without looking under it first just in case the Devil lurked there, for superstition says he has a penchant for hiding in that particular spot!

Because, as I mentioned at the start of this chapter, much attention is given to protecting the entrances to the house, there is conversely danger in certain instances over things that might cause luck to leave. For example, china ornaments of animals should never be placed so that they face a door for they will allow the luck to run out of the house. This belief has developed from the old association of objects, for once a man's prosperity was judged by possessions such as sheep and cattle and should they look in his direction then wealth was adjudged to be coming his way, while if they looked elsewhere then luck could not reach him. From this it is only a step to the thought that representations of such animals might harbour the same good fortune if made to face the household. Similarly it is widely believed to be unlucky to sweep any dust or waste material directly *out* of the house, for this could carry your good luck away with it. The superstitious housewife should sweep such waste into the centre of the room, collect it up in a pan and then carry the lot out of doors to avoid any repercussions.

Brushes and brooms have a place in our story, too, the main reason being the old belief that witches used brooms to fly on for their missions of evil, or to ride to the meeting with their master the Devil, known as the Sabbat. As far as a new broom is concerned, it should always be used the first time to sweep something *into* the house, thereby symbolically bringing luck into the place. It is not a good idea to buy a new brush of any kind in the month of May: this superstition appears to have originated with the Romans, who decreed May as the month of death, and said that to gather broom, which they believed was a magical plant of phallic significance, might well endanger the life of the man who performed the act. The phallic significance is also evident in an English country belief that a young girl who walks over a broomstick will become pregnant before she marries. With the passage of time the old Roman superstition has evolved into the following rhyme still widely repeated:

If you buy a broom or brush in May
You'll sweep the head of the household away.

True or not, the brush has swept us neatly through the last of the household superstitions and out into the even more surprising and mysterious lore of the garden and countryside beyond.

Just in case you should still be sceptical about breaking a mirror – a cutting from *The Daily Mail* of 25 September 1978

NOBODY believes the old wives' tale about broken mirrors bringing ill fortune—nobody except several thousand Philadelphians stuck in a memorable traffic jam. The jam happened when container truck split open, decanting and shattering about four tons of . . . yes, mirrors.

CHAPTER 4

THE LORE OF
EARTH AND SKY

An old craftsman making
corn dollies which
superstition says should be
woven from the last straws of
the harvest. The Corn Spirits
then live in them until the
next year, when in return for
such kindness they will
ensure another good harvest

THE LORE OF EARTH AND SKY

Superstition maintains that if the Aurora Borealis is seen in either Britain or America it is a portent of war. This happened in 1939 when the Northern Lights, as the display is also called, were seen as far south as London; and in America, just prior to the attack on Pearl Harbor, they were seen on three successive nights as far south as Cleveland, Ohio

The powers of nature have always been something of a mystery to man. There is still much that baffles us even in our scientifically advanced age, and it is not surprising that primitive man was almost terrified by the inexplicable forces he found all around him. Predictably, he invested many of them with capabilities they never had, but equally he developed beliefs that while we might similarly wish to dismiss them, have come down to us in deeply rooted superstitions. For instance, trees and plants have been seen as the dwelling place of spirits, animals as the custodians of knowledge of the future, and the weather elements as signs of good and evil. Indeed such was the reverence people as late as the Romans accorded to their land, and in particular their gardens, that they placed them under the protection of great gods and goddesses, and erected statues to mark this fact. Today we unconsciously continue this belief by dotting our lawns or flowerbeds with small gnomes or other figures believed to be bringers of good luck.

As the weather is one of the first things that concerns us on leaving the house it makes a good starting point. The earliest men believed that evil spirits brought bad weather and beneficent gods the good, and from this standpoint many of the superstitions we

Eclipses have terrified mankind until quite recent times and given rise to numerous superstitions. This eighteenth-century engraving shows an eclipse of the moon observed in Peru

now come across evolved, some mixed with observation over many years and a few even having some scientific credibility about them. Take the popular verse which runs:

Red sky at night – shepherd's [sailor's] delight,
Red sky in the morning – shepherd's [sailor's] warning.

Meteorological science informs us that the red hue means the atmosphere is relatively dry and there is dust in the air – not conditions likely to cause rain. So when the sun sets in the west the red reflection comes from clouds that have passed by and therefore cannot cause rain; in the morning the position is reversed when the sun appears in the east and causes a red glow on the clouds on the west, those coming in our direction.

The sun has been worshipped since primitive times, and superstition is wise in saying that it is ill-omened to look or point at the sun for this shows disrespect: a direct look at the sun will certainly damage the eyes. The old idea that when darkness fell across the face of the sun disaster was imminent has now been proved to be incorrect for we know such events are caused by eclipses. In this context I might mention here that the belief it is unlucky to open an umbrella indoors originated through sun worship in the East; so as not to offend the sun these earliest of shades were shaped in its image and only royalty was allowed to use them, and with the passage of time the superstition developed that it was courting misfortune by insulting the sun if they were opened anywhere but in the open air.

67

The Coggia comet of 1874, which passed so close to the earth that there were fears it would actually hit the planet

The moon likewise has been held in awe since time immemorial, and the claim that the full moon can turn people mad – the word lunatic having derived from the word for moon, *luna* – is based on the superstition that such people have offended the goddess of night. The time of the new moon is a good moment for judging future weather: country lore says if the 'horns' of the moon point slightly upwards then the month will be fine, but if the outline of the whole moon can be seen there is rain ahead. It is a good idea to bow to the new moon and turn over any money you may have in your pocket for this will lead to it being doubled before the month is out, and in America it is claimed a young girl can find out about her future love life if she looks at the new moon over her right shoulder and repeats this verse:

New moon, true moon, white and bright,
If I am to have a lover, let me dream of him tonight.
If I am to marry far, let me hear a bird cry,
If I am to marry near, let me hear a cow low,
If I am to marry never, let me hear a hammer knock.

The stars, too, have been regarded with awe by man from primitive times and today they form the basis of a whole 'industry' based on astrology and fortune-telling which needs no discussing here. Shooting stars are particularly lucky and a wish made when you see one will be granted.

Comets, though, have usually been regarded with alarm, being regarded as an omen of disaster such as earthquakes or plagues, or the death of a ruling monarch. Halley's Comet appeared just before the Batttle of Hastings which resulted in the death of King Harold, and it is said that one was seen in the heavens when Queen Elizabeth I lay dying, a fact her attendants tried unavailingly to keep from her.

As we can see, these beliefs stem from man's idea that the heavens were where the gods lived, and it is interesting to hear people still referring to 'the Man in the Moon' although we have been there and found he does not exist. Another belief every bit as ancient, which has stood the test of time, is the claim of people suffering from arthritis and rheumatism that they can tell rain is on the way when they get more pain than usual in their joints. Study has proved that a decrease in atmospheric pressure or a rise in humidity does produce certain effects on the body and I have read accounts of arthritic people being in considerable agony before sudden floods like those in Devon and Essex a few years back.

Unexpected activity on the part of certain animals is also held to be an indication of a change in the weather, rain in particular, and

One of George Cruikshank's amusing sketches illustrating the superstition about St Swithun

we shall come to specific examples of this when dealing with creatures in general. Perhaps the most interesting of weather superstitions is the claim that if it rains on 15 July, St Swithun's Day, then it will rain for forty days thereafter. The origin of this belief takes us back to the ninth century and a bishop named Swithun who specifically requested to be buried outside his church in Winchester. When, a century later, he was canonised and his body was about to be moved inside the church as a token of respect, a terrible storm broke out on the day work should have begun – 15 July 971 – and continued unabated for forty days. To the superstitious people of the time this seemed a clear indication that the saint did not want to be removed from his humble resting place and so his body was left where it was. Should any rain fall on 15 July, it is taken that St Swithun is reminding everyone not to attempt such foolishness again, and keeping the bad weather up for the same period just to underline the message. (Incidentally, meteorological study of the period over many years has shown that it *is* more subject to unsettled weather than any other period of the year.)

THE LORE OF EARTH AND SKY

Benjamin Franklin whose discovery of the lightning rod dispelled many of the superstitions about this wild electrical force

A terrible thunderstorm accompanied the death of Cromwell and seemed to substantiate an old superstition.

Left: The Empire State building, New York, which puts paid to the superstition that lightning never strikes the same place twice – it is regularly struck more than fifty times a year!

Because rain plays such an important part in man's life, being essential for himself and his animals and to make his crops grow, tribal groups from the very earliest times employed 'rain-makers' who were supposed to have the power to make it rain. These apparent magicians usually conducted rituals which imitated rain, such as sprinkling water on the ground or pretending to be clouds, but those who were most successful undoubtedly read the signs in nature all around them. Not surprisingly because of its importance, superstition credits rain water with special curative properties such as relieving sore eyes and helping young children to speak.

Lightning, believed by the ancients to be a sign of the wrath of the gods, has attracted many superstitions over the years, the majority of which disappeared after the invention of the lightning rod by Benjamin Franklin. However, in rural areas it is still said that no one is killed by lightning when asleep, and to be awakened by a streak is a good omen. The thorn tree is said to provide immunity from lightning and in Japan I am told the people believe a mosquito net also offers safety. One superstition that is manifestly false is the claim that 'lightning never strikes the same place twice' for when I was last in New York I was told that the Empire State Building is regularly struck more than fifty times every year. The sound of thunder which accompanies lightning has only one surviving superstition attached to it: that when it is heard in winter it signifies the death of a famous person. Perhaps the most quoted example to substantiate this claim is the terrible thunderstorms in 1658 when Oliver Cromwell died and many people believed it was the sound of the Devil coming for his own.

The rainbow, which can bring such a beautiful conclusion to a storm, has naturally always been considered a good omen and it is very common to find people making a wish when they see one. The old legend that a crock of gold is to be found at the end of a rainbow is still passed from mother to child, although English country folk have more faith in using it as a weather omen: one that appears in the afternoon is a sign that the following day will be fine, but if you see it in the morning, watch out for an unsettled tomorrow.

The many superstitions attached to plants are due to two major factors, the reverence which man has always attached to growing things and the fact that they provided him with his earliest calendar, indicating the changing seasons long before he had any specific method of recording them. We accord a special tribute to those gardeners who seem able to grow anything by saying they have 'green fingers' – and this seems to have evolved from those early days when most plants and flowers were believed to be the abodes of elemental spirits; these spirits, like the gods themselves, could tell a sympathetic soul from an unsympathetic one. I have heard people in several parts of Europe say you should always be careful of anyone in whose hands flowers quickly fade or shed their petals.

Almost every flower has some superstition attached to it and there is just not enough space to mention more than a few of the more well-known ones. As a general rule it is considered good luck to give flowers to someone (a tradition begun by the ancient Egyptians), but any flower that blooms out of season should never be brought indoors. Heavily scented flowers (such as the lilac), are said to be suggestive of funerals, while white flowers should never be given to anyone who is sick. Red flowers, roses in particular, are very appropriate for anyone who is ill for they represent blood (also for brides in their bouquets): but it is not a good idea to have a mixture of just red and white flowers in the home for these are associated with the Roman practice of scattering red and white blooms on the graves of lovers and are consequently believed to be unlucky. Purple flowers are said to attract financial luck into a home, and golden or yellow flowers like marigolds, representing the sun, shine good fortune into any room of the house where they are put. Sunflowers are also supposed to bring good luck to any

Certain herbs have long been esteemed for their medicinal properties. Many were used for making tea that had a tonic value

garden where they are planted, and the Welsh say it is lucky to find the first daffodil of Spring as this will bring you more gold than silver in the coming year. The beautiful lily is regarded as a symbol of virginity and it is widely believed that it is most unlucky for a man to damage or spoil one, as this endangers the purity of the womenfolk in his family.

Many wild flowers, too, have superstitions associated with them, such as the buttercup which every child is taught to hold under their chin to see if it gives off a yellow glow indicating they like butter. Both dandelions and daisy heads can be used by young girls to predict their love lives: the number of blows it takes to remove all the seed heads from a dandelion will tell her how many years before she marries, while by plucking the petals from a daisy and reciting the words 'He loves me, he loves me not' she will get the answer about the state of her boyfriend's affections. Both plants also indicate when bad weather is on the way by closing their petals. It came as a surprise to me to discover that both poppies and violets are considered unlucky flowers: of the poppy it is said to be courting misfortune to bring one into the house because they cause illness and if you stare into the centre of one you may go blind (perhaps the reason for this is the narcotic properties of some varieties of the plant). Violets must only be taken into the house in bunches, never singly or they will bring bad luck; and if these pretty flowers should suddenly bloom in the autumn then someone living close by is near death. Snowdrops, too, have the reputation of being harbingers of death if taken indoors, but as they flower at the time when illness is most prevalent this is perhaps not so much of a surprise.

Among the herbs, parsley and mint are both considered lucky though misfortune will strike the family of any gardener who gives away their roots. No woman should ever be allowed to sow parsley unless she is anxious to become pregnant, for as the old saying repeats, "Sow parsley, sow babies"; and mint is said to grow and flourish only on the land of somebody destined to become wealthy.

Rosemary has long been esteemed for its magical and medicinal properties and because of its persistent odour is said to be an aid to a good memory, as Shakespeare remarks in *Hamlet* (Act IV, scene 5) when Ophelia says:

There's rosemary – that's for remembrance
Pray you, love, remember; and there's pansies –
That's for thoughts.

In the light of recent research many of these horticultural super-stitions have proved not to be so ridiculous as they at first seem, for

The mandrake plant which, according to superstition, takes on both male and female form and is extremely difficult to remove from the ground, shrieking like a baby when it is dug up. These illustrations are from Johannes de Cuba's book *Hortis Sanitertis*

scientific tests have shown that certain flowers and leaves do seem to respond to the emotional and physical atmosphere around them, and some plants, such as roses, have actually shown symptoms of distress when harmed or burnt. Indeed on both sides of the Atlantic there have been a spate of articles and books urging us to lavish the same care and affection on our plants that we do on humans if we want them to really flourish. A Russian has even advanced the theory that plants can actually communicate with each other.

In the vegetable garden the hold of superstition continues unabated. The potato has always been considered a good cure for rheumatism if one that has turned hard and black is carried in the pocket. An easy way of ensuring a good crop is for every member of the family to taste the first bunch of new potatoes pulled from the ground, and you can make a wish while doing so. Although it is not very common these days, the mandrake, which is a member of the potato family, has a special place in superstition because of its almost human appearance. It was much valued by herbalists for use in their preparations, but was not easy to take from the ground as it was supposed to give a terrible shriek almost like that of a baby when pulled from the soil.

The cabbage is said to be a lucky vegetable to have in the garden, especially if one is found growing double from a single root, and the lettuce is believed to have aphrodisiac powers. So, too, is the tomato, once known as 'the love apple'. The flowers of bean plants have for centuries been associated with death, for they are said to contain the souls of the dead and that accidents are most likely to happen when they are in bloom. In England, to find a broad bean that is white instead of green is an omen of death in the family. A pea pod that contains only one pea, though, is very lucky, just as is one that contains nine, and in either instance you should take one of the peas and throw it over your right shoulder making a wish as you do so.

Because of its strong taste and smell the onion has been credited with great protective powers. An onion kept in the room where someone is lying sick is said to help drive off the disease, and medical science has admitted that there is some truth in this for a fresh slice of it does seem to attract germs. To rub the juice of the vegetable on your body is said to protect it from pain when struck (many generations of schoolboys have done this on their behinds when a caning was imminent!), and the Welsh in particular used to rub leeks all over their bodies before going into battle for added strength. Garlic similarly possesses the power to keep evil spirits at bay, and a strand of the bulbs hung across the doors or window of a

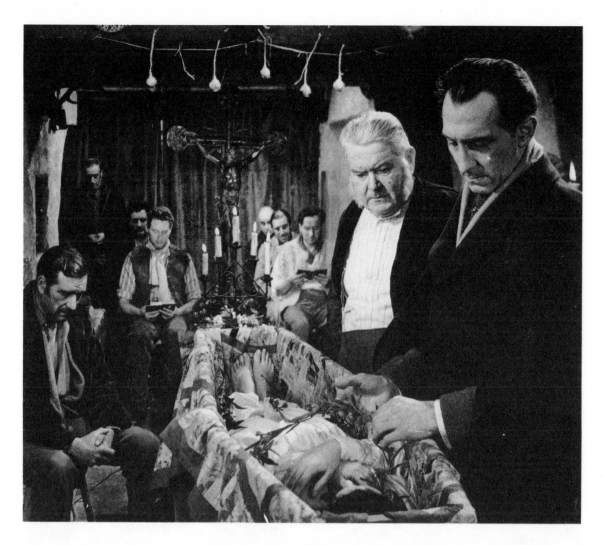

A string of garlic hung in a room will keep vampires at bay according to tradition. A still from the film *The Brides of Dracula*

house will keep vampires at bay – as recent horror films about the activities of the undead have graphically shown. That master of the undead, the Devil, is associated in superstition with the blackberry bush, and in many parts of Europe it is believed the fruit got its colour from being spat upon by the Evil One. Like other fruits, though, in Britain it is said you are in for some good luck if you find a blackberry growing double and share it with anyone else you wish to see prosper.

A good many of the superstitions that are found about trees can be traced back to Greek and Roman times when certain varieties were believed to be the dwelling place of gods and wood spirits. An exception from this rule is the oak which seems to have received its greatest honour at the hands of the Celts and the Druids who believed it had magical qualities and that bad luck would attack anyone who chopped one down. If the tree's leaves do not appear until after those of the ash tree then the summer will be wet, as this old verse explains:

Burrow.

The Druids believed the oak tree had magical qualities and instigated the superstition that it was bad luck to chop one down

Opposite: A recent newspaper report from *The Daily Mail* which demonstrates the continuing observation of tree superstitions

If the ash is out before the oak,
Then we're going to have a soak.
But if the oak's before the ash,
Then we'll only get a splash!

The ash tree is said to have curative properties because of a legend that the first man was created from it. One of its leaves with an equal number of small leaflets on it is said to be lucky and should be carried with you always, and if by any chance the winged seeds fail to appear then this is an omen of the forthcoming death of the monarch. It is extremely unlucky to take any of the flowers from the hawthorn tree indoors for a death will surely result; the origin of this superstition is bound up with the legend that it was the thorns from this tree that were used to make the crown placed on Christ's head when he was crucified. The blood-red berries it

'Lopping at Midnight', an old custom in Epping Forest which sprang from superstitions concerning various trees

produces in autumn are also said to be in memory of this terrible association. Despite this the tree can ward off evil spirits if a branch is hung over the doorway, and it serves as a weather indicator for it will not begin to flower in the spring until the last frost has passed.

Several other trees have associations with the Christian religion. The aspen, for example, is said to have got its famous trembling leaves because wood from it was used for the cross, while the elder is thought to have been the tree from which Judas hung himself. Neither of these trees should be used for firewood, although in the case of the aspen there is a little luck attached to it in that it cannot be struck by lightning. In Wales there is a superstition that no juniper tree should be cut down unless you wish to risk death within the year: again the tree is believed to be under special protection because it played a part in concealing the baby Jesus when his parents were on the run from King Herod's soldiers.

Daily Mail, Monday, November 7, 1977

Woodman Brian braves curse of gipsy tree

By STEPHEN OLDFIELD

TREE doctor Brian Crawford put on a brave face last night after tampering with a beech which carries an ancient curse.

In its 200-year history only two other men have done what he did—lop off some of the tree's branches. One lost his leg soon afterwards, the other his arm.

Brian, 43, took the precaution of calling in the local vicar to conduct a service for his safety.

The beech, which dominates the back garden of Mr Brian Davies in Church Lane, Sale, Cheshire, has a chilling history.

The house was formerly a rectory. Legend has it that the tree was planted in 1780 by the 100-year-old gipsy wife of the rector of St. Martin's Church, Sale, the Rev. Poperwell Johnson.

With it went her curse: that anyone who interfered with the tree, which was in memory of a dead daughter, would meet disaster.

Aged locals still tell of the two men—a railway worker and an engineer — who tumbled out of the local pub 60 years ago, determined to put the story to the test.

Caution

They lopped off two limbs. Within days, the railwayman lost his leg, the other his arm, in accidents at work. Since then, it has been treated with extreme caution.

But two centuries of neglect have taken their toll of the tree. Its lower branches have spread into neighbouring gardens, and Mr Davies decided something had to be done, curse or no curse.

He called in the local council, they consulted the Arboricultural Association, and the Northwich Forestry firm for which Brian works was nominated.

Brian, the forestry manager, did the job with two young workmates. He said last night at his home in Chestnut Close, Cuddington: 'I don't plan to take any special precautions now.

'I'm just trying to regard it as part of the day's work. Though it was reassuring having the vicar in to keep any evil at bay.

'The tree certainly needed attention, what wouldn't after 200 years?'

'We removed some dead wood and one or two limbs, and treated a cavity which turned out much worse than first seemed.'

Prayers

The vicar, the Rev. Stanley Elliot, whose St Martin's Church is 100 yards from the tree, said: 'This legend is taken very seriously by many folk. After all, for some people the word of a gipsy is gospel.

'My service was very simple. I said two or three prayers asking that no harm should come to the men.'

Mr Davies has lived in the house with the cursed beech for 25 years. He said: 'I didn't know about its history when I moved in. I have not done any work on it since.

'I would not have touched it. After all, you never know.'

He added: 'It is strange, but the tree has a curious mood about it. Children play around it, but they have never carved their names on it. People just leave it alone.'

ON·CHRISTMAS·EVE·

The traditional custom of
wassailing fruit trees, as
depicted in *The Windsor
Magazine*, Christmas, 1901

The laurel's reputation for protection and divination – and its use for rewarding victors – no doubt stems from the great admiration in which it was held by the Ancient Greeks and Romans who considered it sacred to Apollo. Its leaves can apparently ward off illness when hung in the house, while if one is thrown on the fire it will reveal what the future holds for you: if it crackles then the signs are good, but not so if it makes no sound. If a branch of the fir tree is damaged in any way by lightning this is an omen of death, and branches of both birch and rowan trees can be used to protect a household if hung over the doorway.

No one needs reminding of the importance of the apple tree and the old maxim that 'an apple a day keeps the doctor away'. The claim may well have originated in Norse legend where it was said the gods retained their youth and strength by eating apples from a tree that grew in the gardens of Asgard. In apple-growing districts of Britain, such as Devon and Somerset, it is still the custom to hold special festivities each winter to encourage the growth of apples in the coming year. These Wassailing Parties are noisy affairs with much cider-drinking and singing and the more rowdy the affair the better the apples are supposed to grow. The toast given to the trees is as follows:

Health to thee, good apple tree,
Well to bear pocket-fulls, hat-fulls,
Peck-fulls, bushel bag-fulls.

Another superstition merely says that the sight of the sun shining through the branches of your apple trees on Christmas day is a sign that you will have a good crop, though it is a bad sign if any apple remains on a tree through the winter to the following spring, for this is an omen that the owner of the orchard will die before the year is out. A plum tree which blossoms in December is also a death omen for the family which owns it. A cherry tree will produce a rich crop if the first cherry is picked and eaten by a woman who has recently given birth to her first child. Nut trees have served frequently in fortune-telling and they also serve as weather prophets because according to old countrymen a big crop of nuts indicates a hard winter, and vice versa, while walnuts for some quite inexplicable reason promise a fine corn harvest when they grow in abundance.

Weeds which blight the gardener's efforts and grow in abundance about our countryside have a curious superstition attached to them that they are God's curse on the earth as a result of Adam's disobedience and that no matter how hard man labours he will never be totally free of them. Interesting, too, is the old belief that nettles were introduced into the British Isles by the Romans who used them to warm their limbs in our cold climate. True or not, country people say that wherever there are nettles you will find dock leaves to ease the pain of their sting. To have the maximum effect, though, you should repeat these words as you rub the parts which have been stung: 'Dock in, nettle out – dock rub, nettle out!'

I finish this chapter with one of the oddest superstitions to do with a plant, which was actually used by the authorities as a propaganda trick: I refer to the humble carrot and an idea that is still widely current that eating them improves the eyesight. During the Second World War the Ministry of Information went to great trouble to let it be known that British pilots were being given a diet based on carrots to help them fly at night. In fact their success in the dark against German targets was brought about by the invention of radar, but the cover story of the carrots was to keep this quiet. (I am told, though, that it is a fact that carrots do contain certain medicinal salts which will help eye troubles.) So it is true to say superstition even played a part in the British war effort!

The custom of apple wassailing continues in strength in the cider orchards of Somerset each year

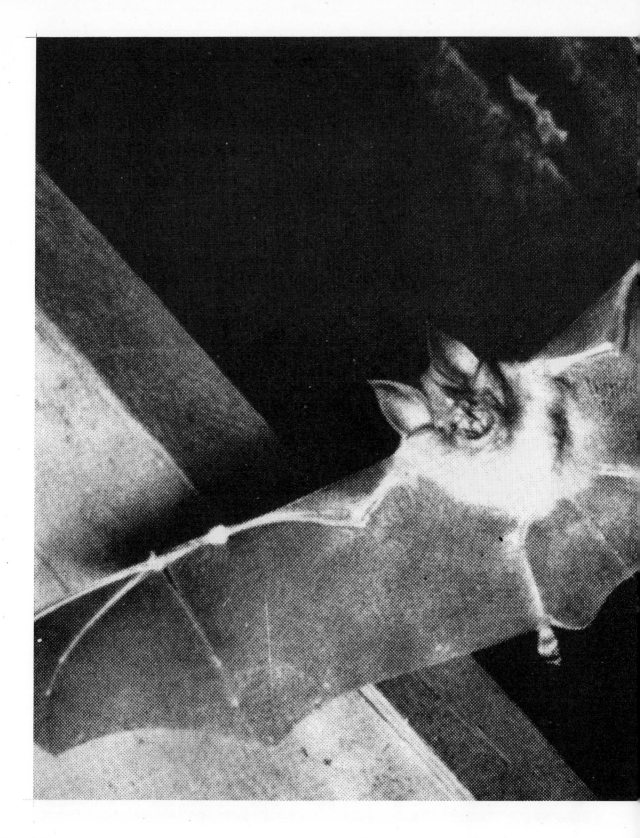

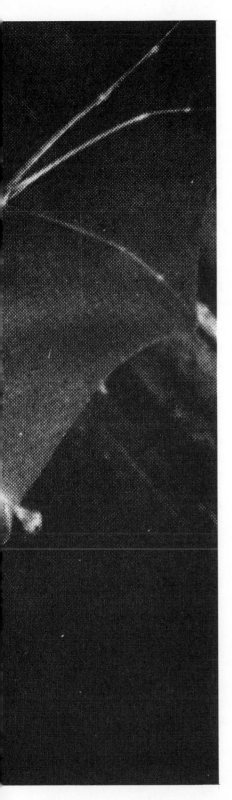

CHAPTER 5

THE SECRET WORLD OF ANIMALS

The sinister appearance of
the bat has made it perhaps
one of the most feared
creatures in superstition, and
whenever it is seen about its
nocturnal activities
something ominous is in
store for the viewer

Man as the highest form of animal life may be lord of all he surveys, but from the earliest days of his dominance he has always credited the other animals with certain qualities beyond his understanding. There is a school of thought that believes animals are psychic, and to understand them you must be psychic yourself. But what is beyond dispute is that they seem to possess supernatural powers which allow, for example, a dog to judge a person's character and a cat to sense weather changes.

Naturally, superstitious ideas have gathered round most animals in abundance and the majority can be traced back to antiquity when many were actually worshipped by man. The cat is, of course, the most famous such example, held in great awe by the Romans and Persians and accorded the position of deity with the name of Bast, the Cat-Goddess, by the ancient Egyptians. No doubt this reverence helps to explain why the feline has enjoyed its special status to this day, and why also during the terrible witch-craft persecutions in the sixteenth and seventeenth centuries its pagan past made it a natural cohort of the devil and witches. (There are legends that witches could change themselves into cats at will.) The cat's renowned tenacity for life similarly enhanced its position and led to the idea it has nine lives.

In the first chapter I mentioned that the black cat was regarded as a harbinger of misfortune virtually everywhere but in the British

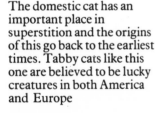

The domestic cat has an important place in superstition and the origins of this go back to the earliest times. Tabby cats like this one are believed to be lucky creatures in both America and Europe

Aside from being man's best friend, the dog has much to tell us about the future, according to superstition. Most particularly, dogs are believed to be able to 'see' death approaching a human being

Isles. For this reason tabby and grey cats are believed to be lucky, especially if such an animal wanders into your home and takes up residence, for this is a sign some money is on its way to you. White cats, which are often strikingly beautiful animals, are also very often deaf and for this reason superstition regards them as creatures to be treated with suspicion. Worldwide, the cat is looked on as an infallible weather forecaster: if one sneezes then rain is on the way; a cat sitting with its back to the fire indicates a storm, while one sharpening its claws on a table leg is a sign of a change in the weather, usually for the better.

'Man's best friend' the dog is not so surrounded by superstition as the cat, but is credited with the extraordinary ability of being able to tell a good person from a bad, invariably backing off, growling, from someone it distrusts. Dogs are supposed to have the power of 'second sight' and can see ghosts as well as sense the death of a human being close to them. Human tissues undergo a chemical change just before death, and it may be that dogs are attuned to this in some way: certainly there is no shortage of examples of dogs howling outside a sick-room or over the body of a master who has been killed or died accidentally. Naturally enough it is said to be an omen of death when a dog is heard howling near any door, while if they whine when a child is born then it will lead an evil life. The sight of a dog eating grass, rolling on the floor or scratching itself excessively are all said to be omens that rain is imminent.

The horse, which has played such an important part in man's development, has always been a prize possession, and the fact that the Greeks worshipped it as a symbol of the goddess, Artemis,

Most horses are considered lucky in superstition – but the pure white horse like this one has special powers

probably accounts for the beliefs which have grown up around it. White horses have always been considered lucky to see or own, and the origin here may well be Tacitus's account of the sacred white horses which were drawn about the countryside to bless the land, attended in state by priests. A horse with 'white stockings' on its front legs is considered lucky, and if these are combined with a star shape on the forehead then doubly so. (Look out for such a beast next time you go racing!) Luckier still is a horse with a groove on its neck into which a thumb can be placed, for superstition calls this 'the Prophet's thumb print' and claims the creature must be descended from one of the five brood mares which belonged to the prophet Mahomet. As a weather omen, horses indicate a storm on the way if they stand in a group with their backs to a hedge.

The cow also has a history of being specially revered, and in India and parts of the East is still regarded as a sacred animal. While in the West we do not treat it with quite the same reverence, superstition says it is lucky to meet a herd of cows on the road, and it seems likely this developed from earlier times when people lived in smaller, isolated communities with infrequent communication, and the arrival of a drover with cattle to provide milk or be sold for meat would be a good sign and ensure food supplies for the inhabitants. In the past cattle were believed to be one of the prime targets of witches and, apart from the numerous charms developed to protect them, it was the custom if a herd was struck by illness to

The cow is regarded as a sacred animal in India and parts of the East, while in Europe the beast can be a lucky omen when met in certain situations

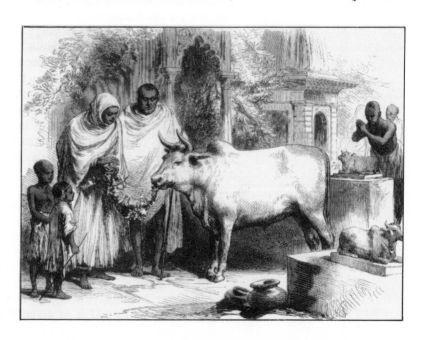

The Devil is often shown with a goat's head which is part of the reason why the superstitious are in some awe of the creature

burn a calf alive because of the maxim 'burn one to save the herd'. When cows lie on high ground it is said to be a sign of good weather to come, while if they feed close together or low excessively then rain is imminent. If a cow breaks into your garden then there will be a death in the family.

The origin of it being lucky to see a herd of sheep originated for much the same reason as for cows. Although the term 'black sheep' is used to refer to a person who does not conform, in many parts of Europe an actual black sheep brings good luck to the flock into which it is born. The same weather conclusions are drawn from the activities of sheep as cows, and there is also an interesting superstition that on Christmas morning all sheep bow three times to the East as they remember their forebears who looked on when Christ was born in the stable in Bethlehem.

In Ireland I heard the extraordinary superstition that pigs can see the wind, but what does seem more likely is that when they are seen hurrying about their stye or carrying a bunch of straw in their mouth then there is a storm on the way. It is unlucky to have a pig cross your path – turn your back until it has gone – and if it begins to make a rather strange whining noise then there is to be a death in the family of its owner.

There are also some queer superstitions about donkeys and there is a general belief throughout Europe that a donkey knows when it is about to die and hides itself away, thus giving rise to the expression 'You'll never see a dead donkey' – and if you do it's a very lucky sight. When a donkey brays and twitches its ears, this is said to be an omen that there will soon be wet weather, and according to superstition the creature got those long ears and its reputation for being stupid when it was in the Garden of Eden. Apparently after Adam had named all the animals, God asked them what their names were, and the poor old donkey could not remember his; Adam pulled its ears unmercifully saying, 'Donkey! Your name is donkey!' The creature was somewhat rehabilitated, another old belief says, when it carried Christ into Jerusalem on Palm Sunday and thereby got the mark of a cross on its back.

Superstition regards the goat with some caution, partly because of the ancient worship of the god Pan who was half-goat and half-man, and partly because one of the tricks attributed to the Devil is the ability to turn himself into a goat. It is doubtless because of this association that drawings of the Devil show him with the horns and cloven hoofs of a goat. I have heard country folk in England say that you can never see a goat a whole day through because at some time during the twenty-four hours he must slip away for a meeting

VILLAGERS near Minsk in Russia get a 24-hour advance warning of rain —from a hare.

"He drums his fore-paws against the trunk

of a certain tree, said mayor Pavel Andreye-vitch.

"Then we know it will rain, even if the sky is still cloudless.

"This hare has never been wrong."

The hare has long been credited with the power of foretelling changes in the weather. This recent example of his ability is from *The News of the World*, 24 September 1978

This old French engraving illustrates the belief that toads once had a precious stone embedded in their heads which only a man of virtue could remove

with his master, the Devil. Perhaps because of these associations we should not be surprised that a goat's foot or some hairs from his beard are believed to be talismans for driving off evil spirits.

Of the wild animals, hares also have a sinister reputation for it was once believed witches had the power to turn themselves into these nimble creatures. A hare running across your path is said to be an ill-omen, but one running ahead of you is a good sign, as Queen Boadicea found when one did just this before she had a successful battle against the Romans. Rabbits are considered lucky and are widely regarded as symbolic of the moon god because of the way they gambol about under a full moon. A rabbit's foot is a very famous good luck charm, and we have the choice of two alternatives for the origin of the idea: one explanation is that their prolific breeding exhibits a creative power automatically associated with prosperity and success; the second is that as rabbits are born with their eyes open they can 'see off' evil right from the time of their birth. If you want a month of good luck there is another old British superstition that on the last day of the month you should say 'rabbits' before going to sleep and then on awakening on the first say 'hares'.

To hear a mouse squeaking anywhere near someone who is ill is a sign that the person will die, and much of the abhorrence towards mice (who are actually far cleaner creatures than generally imagined) probably stems from the old superstition that they are the souls of people who have been murdered. If they nibble anyone's clothing during the night, that person will suffer some misfortune, while no journey undertaken after seeing one is likely to be successful. Frogs, also, are said to be the souls of children who have died and consequently it is very unlucky to kill one.

There is a curious legend in Europe that it is impossible to catch a weasel asleep, and superstition says it is bad luck if one crosses your path and appears near your home making its distinctive squeaking sound. A fox passing your home is also a forerunner of misfortune, and it is not a good thing to see a wolf or speak the word 'wolf' during December lest you run the risk of being attacked by one. In Canada, though, the beast does not have such a sinister reputation, and a string of wolf's teeth worn around the neck is said to be a protection against evil spirits. The bear, which also roams the North American continent, is looked on with favour in many parts, although there is a superstition among American back-woodsmen that bears only mate once every seven years, and when they do they cause such a disturbance in the atmosphere that any pregnant cattle in the district will give birth to still-born calves.

The bat is perhaps the one animal above all others about which it

The bear is regarded as a creature of good luck throughout the North American continent

Even domestic pets have retained their ancient power to sense imminent disaster – as this report from *The Sunday Express* of 10 December 1978 clearly shows

THE PETS WHO KNEW THE EARTH WAS GOING TO QUAKE

VILLAGERS were astonished when deer wandered down from the hills and stood staring at them in apparent bewilderment.

Also when every pet cat left home, some carrying kittens, and did not return for two days.

Dogs barked, fowl broke out of chicken runs, and rats and mice scurried about on the open ground.

It was a cloudless spring day. Nobody was expecting trouble. Then suddenly the earth shook, buildings fell, and people ran for their lives.

The earthquake that hit Friuli, in northern Italy, in May 1976, was widespread although casualties were light. But research has shown that a large number of animals sensed its onset.

78 reports

And a report in Britain's science journal, Nature, suggests that they were affected by a build-up of atmospheric electricity just before the upheaval.

is easy to understand why superstitions have so readily developed. Its sinister appearance, its nocturnal activities and eerie, chilling cry make it a creature to startle even the bravest soul, especially because of its association with vampires. The poet Virgil also helped to establish the bat's reputation by identifying it with the winged monsters of Homeric legend. Not surprisingly it is considered bad luck to kill one, and it is a death omen if one flies into a house. If one flies past you then watch out for someone is trying to deceive you; and if any are seen on the wing before their normal time of twilight good weather is on the way. I cannot vouch for two other suggestions, that it is lucky to keep a bone from a bat in your pocket or that the right eye of a bat will make you invisible, but I can categorically deny the old belief that if a bat flies into a woman's hair it will become entangled and have to be cut free: it has been tested scientifically and even in the longest hair the creature still got free. What brave women they must have been to have taken part in such an experiment!

There are even more superstitions attached to birds than to animals, but we have only space to consider a cross-section here.

Icarus, the first in an
unending line of men who
have tried to imitate the bird

Man has, of course, always envied the bird's ability to fly, and since
the time of Icarus has vainly tried to imitate it. In his admiration he
has also seen many signs in the activities of birds, and the Greeks,
for instance, made a science of this called Ornithomancy. Two of
the most widespread superstitions are that birds coming into or
very close to a house portend a death therein, while to see a flight of
birds just before you set off on a journey will lead to a successful
trip.

Hens seem to head the list of domestic birds, and wherever they
are kept it is quite common to hear people recite the lines:

A whistling woman and a crowing hen
Are neither good for God nor men.

It is difficult to establish the reason for this idea, but a much
older version of the rhyme I found has a second line which reads,
'Will frighten the Devil out of his den', so presumably it was once

Right: Chickens and hens
have always featured in
superstition and there is
much they can tell us about
the future

Left: The terrifying vampire
bat, which according to
tradition feeds on the blood
of both animals and humans.
A still from the film *Kiss of
the Vampire*

The peacock heralds rain when it makes its harsh calling sound, according to superstition. Its feathers, though, should never be taken indoors for, as this illustration from Thomas Bewick's *History of British Birds* (1847) shows, they are said to be symbolic of the 'evil eye'

felt too much chatting or crowing was likely to upset Old Nick and bring him on to the scene to put a stop to the disturbance. In any event, superstition says both are unlucky, and there is a distinct likelihood that even if the Devil does not appear the weather at least will change.

A hen that crows near a house is supposed to be forecasting a death, and any hen that persistently crows is said by countryfolk to have got 'the Devil in her' and should be killed before she takes to destroying her eggs and teaches the other birds to do the same. Incidentally it is said to be unlucky if a hen lays an even number of eggs, and you would be well advised to remove one from a sitting bird. The cock is highly regarded because from the earliest times it was believed that when he crowed to welcome the dawn all ghosts and evil spirits had to return to the underworld. A cock crowing in the evening is an omen of bad weather the following day, and if it calls during the night hours there is going to be a death in the family. Shakespeare records another interesting superstition about the cock in *Hamlet*, that the bird crows all through Christmas Eve to Christmas morning so that no evil spirits can spoil this holy time.

Ducks and geese are said to indicate wind and rain on the way when they hiss and quack more than usual. A duck that lays dun-coloured eggs is very ill-omened and should be destroyed, according to an old English belief, and while legends tell us that geese are particularly silly birds, if one flies around the house it is said to know that death is on the way.

Those lovely birds swans and peacocks also feature in superstition. The swan was dedicated to Apollo, the Greek god of music, which may account for the belief which has developed that when one of the birds is dying it sings, thus giving rise to the expression 'swansong'. Actually the bird makes its usual hissing sound, but there is still much faith in the belief that when one of them lays its head and neck back over its body during the daytime then a storm is on the way. Like the swan, the peacock is looked on as a 'royal' bird but its feathers should never be brought indoors for decoration as they are unlucky. The explanation for this is most likely the eye symbol on the feathers which is seen as symbolic of the 'evil eye'. The peacock is another indicator of rain, signalling its approach with a harsh crying call.

The pigeon, as the last of the domestic birds, has attracted little superstition, though a lone white one perching on a chimney is said to be a death omen. For quite a time when feather beds were popular, it was claimed that pigeon feathers in such a bed only prolonged the agonies of someone dying, and consequently any

The much loved robin redbreast, which superstition says it is very unlucky to kill. From Bewick's *History of British Birds*

pillow or mattress containing them was invariably removed from a sick-room.

Wild birds, too, fall into the category of lucky or unlucky; let us look at the lucky ones first. I have always thought the superstition about the blackbird is among the most extraordinary, for it claims if two males are seen sitting together this is a very good omen: it certainly should be when you consider how each blackbird claims his bit of territory and drives off all others. Should a blackbird nest anywhere in your house then you can look forward to a year of good fortune.

The robin is perhaps the most loved of all wild birds and dire are the omens if you should kill one. The story that it was a robin who covered the unfortunate 'Babes in the Wood' with leaves to help them keep warm has done much to endear it to children everywhere. Legend has it that it got its distinctive red breast when it tried to pull the bloody thorns from Christ's head as he hung on the cross. The bird has also been regarded as sacred to the household gods since the earliest times, and William Blake in his poem, *Auguries of Innocence*, insists:

A Robin Redbreast in a Cage
Puts all Heaven in a Rage.

A blackbird making its nest in the roof of a house – as this one did in Essex – is said to bring good luck to the occupants

The swallow, the 'herald of summer', who got his name according to superstition through trying to cheer up Christ while he was on the Cross

Although today the wren is almost as popular as the robin, it was for many years hunted and killed, partly out of hatred (because it was regarded as a sacred bird by the Druids and consequently denounced by the early Christians) and partly because it was believed the bird's feathers would prevent anyone from drowning and naturally there was a good trade to be had in them among seafaring folk. Perhaps by way of redress it has now become accepted in superstition that it is very unlucky for a sailor to kill one.

The swallow is another favourite bird and this is not difficult to understand when one remembers its arrival heralds summer. Any house on which it builds its nest is due for good luck, and in particular protection from fire and storm. When they fly low it is a signal for rainy weather. According to a Danish story, the bird got its name because one flew above the cross on which Christ was crucified, crying 'Svale! Svale!' (Cheer up! Cheer up!) and because of this became known as the *svale* or swallow. The pretty dove is sacred, too, and tradition claims it is the one bird into which the Devil cannot transform himself. Its association with love has come about because it was believed to be the messenger of Venus, although among miners it is considered ill-omened and no superstitious miner would go underground after seeing one flying near the pitshaft. The stork, of course, has always been seen as the deliverer of babies, and this belief no doubt originated from its well-known devotion to its own young. Superstition says the sight of a stork flying over a house indicates a pregnancy is imminent, while if a pair nest in the vicinity not only will your life be enriched but your animals and crops will flourish.

The raven is a most ill-omened bird in superstition, and is celebrated in Edgar Allan Poe's famous poem, 'The Raven'. This illustration is by Henry Anelay (1875)

The kingfisher is another very lucky bird, and to carry some of its feathers on your person is both a protection and a charm for good fortune. I have heard a story that it got its beautiful plumage because when Noah freed the animals from the Ark after the deluge, the kingfisher was the first bird to fly away and thus got the red of the setting sun on its breast and the azure of the sky on its back. There is an equally interesting legend attached to the cuckoo, whose first call in the spring provides annual reports in the correspondence column of *The Times*. Apparently from early times the number of calls a cuckoo made indicated different things whether you were a young person (the time when you would marry), a married couple (the arrival of your next child), or old folk (how much longer you had to live), and it is said that because the poor bird was kept so busy answering such enquiries, it had no time to build a nest and therefore had to offload its young on to foster-parents. Nonetheless, it is a lucky bird and it is widely believed that whatever state of health you are in at the time you hear the first call, so you will remain for the rest of the year. And a wish made at this time is supposed to come true.

Of the ill-omened birds, the raven has surely the worst character, and his ability to predict the future, in particular death, has led to some famous superstitions. Perhaps the best known of these concerns the ravens in the Tower of London and the belief

that if they should be lost or fly away then the Royal Family will die and Britain will fall to an enemy. The American Indians call the raven 'the messenger of death' and it seems that as it has a very developed sense of smell it can sense the odour of decay from some distance, so that when it appears in the vicinity a death is believed to be imminent. The whole ominous nature of this creature is marvellously evoked in Edgar Allan Poe's poem entitled 'The Raven'.

The rook also has an unsavoury reputation, though not universally. Should a group of them leave an area where they have settled then a human connected with that land is about to die. As their nests are usually very visible, they are believed to be an omen of the summer weather to come: if they are high up it will be fine, but low down it will be cold and wet. The crow, too, has few friends and for centuries has been associated with witchcraft. If one flies around the house or perches alone this is an omen of misfortune or death; and should a flock of them suddenly abandon a wood where they have been nesting there are going to be hard times ahead. The same omens are often accorded to the magpie, and I have come across old countrymen in Britain who believe the best way to avoid bad luck when the bird is around is to take off your hat as it passes. The reason for misfortune being associated with it is because it was the only bird which would not enter the Ark, but preferred to remain on its own outside. It is also held in awe because it is one of the very few wild creatures that is coloured black and white – a combination of the Devil's colour and the sacred or holy colour of white.

The jackdaw is a mixture of good and bad: one of them perching on a building is a sign of misfortune, but if a whole group does so then both an addition to the family and an increase in its financial wealth are signified. The little sparrow, too, is considered ill-omened in some parts of the world, though by and large he seems quite popular. His peculiar hopping run when on the ground is said to have been his punishment for chirping 'He's alive, he's alive' during the Crucifixion and thereby encouraging the Romans to torture Christ. A group of sparrows chirping excitedly are said to be an omen of rain.

Lastly, we come to the owl, who no doubt earned his ill-repute because of his solitary, nocturnal existence – although mankind has attributed to him special knowledge which we recognize in the saying 'a wise old owl'. It is unlucky to see one by daylight and one flying around the house hooting at night is a signal of death. Among the more curious beliefs about the bird are that a person who looks into an owl's nest will thereafter be a sad and morose soul, while the sound of one hooting among houses is a sign that an

A superb photograph of a barn owl with a field vole it has just caught. According to superstition if an owl flies round a house at night it is an omen that someone inside is shortly going to die

Despite the revulsion felt by many people towards spiders, they are the subject of numerous good luck superstitions. And as this picture shows they are actually kept as pets by Brazilian children!

unmarried girl has just lost her virginity. In America, the whip-poor-will is held in similar awe and its cry heard near a house at night is the sign of an imminent death.

Of all ground creatures, the spider has probably had more different superstitions attached to it than any other. It is certainly a prime ingredient in innumerable old cures for illness, and you can expect very bad luck indeed if you should kill one, for as an old proverb says:

If you wish to live and thrive
Let the spider run alive.

Although many theories have been advanced as to the origin of beliefs about spiders, most can be traced back to the Middle Ages, when the healthiest households were those full of spiders. In those insanitary times, flies carried disease everywhere, and only in the places where spiders were to be found in abundance could you hope to have immunity from such pests and thereby prosper. It is a good omen to see a spider spinning its web (you will shortly get some new clothes), and if one drops on your face or clothes – particularly the little red variety known as the 'money spider' – then your finances are about to improve. A web also has the power to stop bleeding when laid over the wound, a quality superstition says it has had ever since one hid the infant Jesus from Herod's soldiers.

I must also devote a little space to insects which have their own considerable list of superstitions. Take the ant, for example, of which superstition says 'stepping on ants brings rain'. Ants also signify bad weather on the way when they are seen to be very agitated; and although it may be a great nuisance to you an ant's nest built near a door of your home is a clear sign of financial security in the future. On the other hand it is a death omen if a beetle walks over your shoe and you are advised not to kill one for this will cause a storm.

Crickets, which were once found about the fireplace, are still seen as omens of death when they come into a house, as John Dryden reported in *Fables, Ancient and Modern* (1699): 'Owls, Ravens, Crickets, seem the wave of death.' However, Gilbert White in his *Natural History and Antiquities of Selborne* (1789) has a kindlier view:

They are the housewife's barometer, foretelling her when it will rain; and are prognostic sometimes, she thinks, of ill or good luck, of the death of a near relation or the approach of an absent lover. By being the constant companions of her solitary hours they naturally become the objects of her superstition.

Bees feature in several old superstitions, and it is still widely believed that if they suddenly swarm on a tree or bush in someone's garden there will be a death in the house soon after

Among flying insects, ladybirds are considered lucky and if one alights on you, you should count the number of spots it has and each one will represent a happy month to come. According to tradition, the little creature is symbolic of the Virgin Mary and this in part explains why children delight in putting a ladybird on their hands and repeating the words, 'Ladybird, ladybird, fly away home – your house is on fire and your children are gone.' Superstition says that the little creature immediately takes off because it actually understands the human tongue – the truth is more mundane: it cannot stand a sweaty palm! Butterflies are believed to contain the souls of dead people, and to see one flying at night is an omen of death. However, should the first butterfly you see in the year be either white or gold then you will have twelve happy months ahead. A moth is a bad luck sign if one flies into your house.

It may seem strange but the common old housefly is actually a luck bringer if one should fall into a glass you are drinking from, and there is even good in that pest the wasp. If you kill the first one you see in any year swiftly enough you will have good luck and not be troubled by your enemies for the rest of that year.

And so, finally, to bees which have amassed a remarkable list of beliefs. Because of their industry and well-ordered existence, not to mention the many uses to which their product, honey, can be put, they have earned a special regard, and it is not unusual to hear them referred to as 'the Little Servants of God', and country people say they should always be told of important events that have happened in the families of their owners, such as birth, marriage or death. They are apparently very conscious of their dignity and it is an ill-omen to give away a hive: the bees must be sold for a fair price commensurate with their worth, and they should never be removed from one place to another without being told beforehand. If they become lazy it is said there will be a disaster shortly, and should they suddenly swarm on a bush or tree there will be a death nearby. I have heard it claimed that bees can tell whether a girl is pure or not, and that any young woman whose family has a hive and who is about to be married should inform the bees before doing so if she wants a long and happy marriage. She must go to the hive and whisper quietly, 'Little Brownies, little Brownies, your mistress is to be wed.' If she wants to make doubly sure of their blessing, she will later leave a piece of wedding cake outside the hive for their enjoyment.

And that brings me to a most appropriate point at which I can leave the secret world of animals and move into the realms of the human heart and the part superstition has played in love and marriage.

CHAPTER 6

THE MYSTIQUE OF LOVE AND MARRIAGE

A guard of honour of musical
instruments for the wedding
of a French conductor keeps
alive an old marriage custom
rooted in superstition

Because the apple was used by the Devil in the temptation of Eve in the Garden of Eden, it has played an important part in love superstitions ever since

Because love, courtship and marriage are such important events in human existence, superstition has made much of all their vagaries and uncertainties. The desire to know what the future holds, particularly among young girls, has been a pressing need from early times, and though today's modern miss will probably not go to quite the lengths her predecessors did, looking for omens in strange rituals or acting in deference to bizarre superstitions, her anxiety for the course of true love to run happily is every bit as strong. Almost all the superstitions recorded in this section attempt to satisfy a young girl's need to know how and where she will find a sweetheart and whether he will become her husband; there are even certain methods for keeping his affection. Young men, on the other hand, seem always to have been more practical and less sentimental, and in consequence there are very few beliefs relating to their role in love-making. Perhaps because of the romantic nature of love itself, it comes as no surprise to find many of the traditions seem quaint and almost ridiculous: nevertheless they persist from generation to generation just as the need for love itself persists.

The apple has always had a prominent part to play in love, probably because it was with one of these fruits that the Devil tempted the first lover, Eve, in the Garden of Eden. Since then uncounted generations of girls have taken an apple, peeled the skin off in a continuous piece and flung it over their left shoulder: superstition has told them that it will fall in the shape of a letter indicating the initial of their lover's Christian name. If it breaks, though, the omens say she will not marry at all. A girl who wants to know the depth of her boyfriend's affections should drop a pip from an apple she has eaten on to the fire and quietly whisper his name. If it goes off with a cracking sound then he is obviously 'bursting' with love for her.

One of the simplest of all love rituals is to take a daisy or dandelion head and pluck or blow the fluffy seeds while repeating, 'He loves me, he loves me not . . .' Equally simple, a young girl can place her shoes in the form of a T before she goes to bed and recite the following verse:

Hoping this night my true love to see,
I place my shoes in the form of a T.

Four engravings from George Cruikshank's humorous and evocative series of sketches about the course of love and marriage entitled 'Whom to Marry'. The illustrations are subtitled, in order from left to right, 'The Young Maid and her Pets', 'Blind-Man's Buff', 'The Declaration' and finally 'The Wedding'

A mirror can be employed to the same end: in America if a young girl holds one over a well she will see reflected in it the face of the man she will wed, while in Britain merely sleeping with one under the pillow will cause her to dream of him.

The hours of darkness seem to have been a favourite time for love rituals, although timid young ladies may have hesitated over such ideas as going to a churchyard at midnight and walking around it twelve times. If you did, it was said you would see the ghostly shape of your future husband. Another superstition says the same result can be achieved by going out into the garden at midnight and picking twelve sage leaves, at which a shadowy form of hubby-to-be will approach from the opposite side of the garden. If the thought of trying either of these on her own was too much for a young girl, she could always recruit a girlfriend for another scheme. The two should sit alone in a room from midnight to one o'clock, and during this time they should pluck as many hairs from their head as their ages and lay them on a linen cloth. As soon as the clock struck one, each should turn over every hair separately saying:

An old eighteenth-century engraving of a young girl seeing the face of her future husband in the mirror as a result of following certain superstitious customs

SECRET WAY TO BEAUTIFUL SKIN.

MOON MAGICK!
BEAUTY BALM.

YOUTH REVEALING.

AGE CONCEALING.

MADE FROM BRITISH WILD FLOWERS & TREE BARKS.
ENTIRELY FREE FROM ANIMAL & CHEMICAL INGREDIENTS.

MAN'S greatest compliment:
" You are bewitching !"

ALL PURPOSE BEAUTY BALM

MAGICK, makes you look younger & happier.
Secretly made for you "Where two streams meet,"
From genuine old MAGICK herbal formula.
CLEANSING-The perfect make-up remover.
NOURISHING-Definitely grows connective tissue.
SMOOTHING-Your skin becomes smooth & supple.

CONFIDENTIAL- (SMOOTHS AGEING LINES.)

SIMPLE FACIAL MODELLING CHART FREE.

Magick is our Business.

SELECTED EXPORT ORDERS WELCOMED. MAKES AN ACCEPTABLE & UNIQUE GIFT.

A modern day advertisement for an ancient potion to make a young girl bewitching

I offer this my sacrifice,
To him most precious in my eyes.
I charge thee now come forth to me,
That I this minute may thee see.

This superstition is said to work best when carried out on the night of 30 November, St Andrew's Day. (There are a number of other love traditions listed under specific days in Chapter 7, 'The Traditions of Special Days'.)

Once a girl had set her sights on a man things got considerably easier. One of the most charming superstitions decrees that a girl should pick two long-stemmed roses, naming one for herself and one for the object of her affections, and before she goes to sleep she should twine the stems together, repeating:

Twine, twine and intertwine,
Let my love be wholly mine;
If his heart be kind and true,
Deeper grow his rose's hue.

If her desires are to be fulfilled, the rose will turn steadily darker in colour. In America I have heard an easier way to make your boy-friend love you: you just need to wink at the largest star you can find before going to bed.

Love-philtres, potions and powders as a means for inspiring and securing the affections of men have been used by women and girls from the days of antiquity, and indeed to this very day both in town and country mysterious compounds are mixed and strange incantations said to influence affections. The ancient Egyptians, for example, used hair and nail clippings mixed with the juices of plants and the blood of animals for just such ends, and today much the same thing goes on under the guise of exotic names. Take the evocative 'Dragon's Blood' for instance which is a vital ingredient in numerous love charms. It is not only used as a method of attraction but also by those who are jealous of their lovers and desire to win back their affections. To do this, the powdered 'Dragon's Blood' (which is actually a gum-resin obtained from the *Pterocarpus Indicus* tree found in the East) is wrapped in a piece of paper and thrown on the fire while the following words are repeated:

May he no pleasure or profit see,
Till he comes back again to me.

Nineteenth-century engraving of three young girls preparing a love potion to win themselves handsome suitors. Such operations had, of course, to be conducted at dead of night when all the rest of the household were asleep!

The kiss, the symbol of love, is surrounded by numerous superstitions. This illustration is by R. Anning Bell (1910)

As a charm to attract a lover, the powder should be mixed together with sulphur, quicksilver and saltpetre and then thrown on the fire, repeating the same words.

The Romans developed a whole range of love potions which included the hairs from a wolf's tail, the bones of a toad, pigeon's blood, the entrails of animals and so on, often mixed in wine to disguise the disgusting taste but said to be most effective in achieving their object. That notorious substance, *cantharides*, or Spanish fly, was at the bottom of many other potions, and its effect has been referred to in several verses including John Gray's *Shepherd's Week*:

These golden flies into his mug I'll throw
And soon the swain with fervent love shall glow.

But whether affection has been fairly won or manipulated, the next step in the process of love is the kiss, and once again superstition has been busy. The special regard we have for kissing is something we have inherited from our earliest ancestors, for they believed the air contained magic powers and thus when men and women kissed each other they performed a sacred act by mingling their breath. The description of kissing as 'spooning', a term which has only recently gone out of favour, originated in Wales. Apparently before they used engagement rings, it was the custom for a young Welshman to present the girl of his choice with a wooden spoon on which he had carved symbols of his love such as knots and initials, and if she accepted this, in the eyes of the community they were engaged. Hence 'spooning' came to mean any show of affection, including kissing and hugging. In many parts of the world it is believed to be unlucky to be kissed by anyone who leans over your shoulder: surely a throwback to earlier days when anything performed from behind left you vulnerable to attack. You might also like to note it is an ill-omen to kiss anyone on the nose, as superstition says this will lead to a quarrel. The 'love bite' is said to be ill-omened because of its association with vampires, and will lead to a couple parting.

Love letters also come under the influence of superstition, and here are just a few of the more widespread beliefs. If your hand trembles while you are writing, this is a sign your lover's affection is strong; but don't risk writing in anything other than ink or you may jeopardize the romance. If you make a blot while you are at work the other person is thinking of you at that moment. Sunday is a bad day on which to post a love letter (it will lead to a quarrel) and it is also unwise to send a letter which is insufficiently stamped. If a girl receives two letters from different lovers in the same post it is

Lucrezia Borgia, who gave weight to the old superstition that the reason for placing the engagement ring on the third finger of the left hand was because it contained a special vein that ran directly from it to the heart!

a sign she will marry neither of them. Finally, it is very bad luck to burn love letters – they must always be torn up unless you want an unhappy life.

The business of getting engaged is beset with traditions, too, and the custom of giving or exchanging rings to mark an engagement goes back to the earliest years of the Christian era. Long before this in some places engagement had been marked by the taking of a piece of gold or silver which was broken in half and shared by couples as a token of their love and intention to marry. The choice of the third finger for the ring seems to have arisen because of the mistaken impression that a special vein ran from it direct to the heart; certainly this is what Sir Thomas Browne, the medical authority, records in his *Lectures* (1860): 'It was chosen because a particular nerve, vein or artery is conveyed thereto from the heart, but as a matter of fact both the Greeks and the Romans attached peculiar virtues to this finger and it was supposed to possess certain medical or healing powers.' As an instance of this, in a record of the betrothal of Lucrezia Borgia in 1493 we are told that her ring was placed on the finger 'whose vein leads to the heart'.

Although there have been many types of engagement ring over the years, the single band set with precious stones has proved the most popular, and superstition claims that there are stones most appropriate for the month in which you become engaged. For instance, the diamond, the most valuable of all whose sparkle was said to have originated in the alchemic fires of love, symbolizes innocence and is the stone for April. The emerald, symbolizing success in love, is for May; the agate, health and long life, for June; the carnelian, a contented mind, July; the sardonyx, for a happy married life, August; the chrysolite, an antidote for depression, September; the opal, hope, October; the topaz, fidelity, for November; the turquoise, prosperity, December; the garnet, truth and constancy, January; the amethyst, sincerity, February; and finally the bloodstone, for courage and presence of mind, March. It is, not surprisingly, very unlucky to lose an engagement ring, and it is an augury for an unhappy married life if the ring becomes loose or breaks before the wedding ceremony.

Tradition has even gone on record as saying that neither long nor very short courtships bode well: a year of courtship plus three months of engagement is said to be ideal. Superstition says it is unlucky to propose on a bus or train or in any public place, and if a young man is interrupted by another girl while he is proposing, this other woman will in the fullness of time become his second wife. A man who is refused three times is better off staying single, while anyone who is proposed to at a dance and does not accept will

A bride and groom in their wedding finery – much of it dictated by superstition! A sketch by Charles Pears from *The Lady's Realm*, 1907

be in for a great deal of bad luck! Nor should any girl in her eagerness to catch a man propose to him, for as an old belief maintains:

The maid who asks a man to wed,
Will come to want and beg for bread.

The marriage ceremony itself, as the highspot of love and courtship, has naturally attracted a multitude of superstitions, many of great antiquity. Pre-eminent among these is the idea that it is unlucky to marry a girl from your own locality, a belief which can be traced back to the tribal days of mankind when it was considered cowardly to marry a girl from your own group (you should have the strength to obtain one by guile or force from another tribe) and because even then man had realized the dangers of inbreeding when he saw what happened to his livestock if fresh 'blood' was not regularly introduced into the ranks. As man slowly became more civilized the custom of carrying off a bride by force gave way to a system of barter, and while this still takes place in certain countries, elsewhere remnants survive whenever there is talk of a girl having made 'a good marriage'. The honeymoon, or 'hiding away' of the man with his new bride, is another reminder of when primitive man needed to seclude his mate until she had accepted her new role.

The idea that May is an unlucky month to wed and June a happy one is another belief that originated with the Romans. May was named after Maia, who apart from being the goddess of fertility was also the patroness of the aged and therefore not a suitable deity to have watching over young lovers, whereas June was named after Juno, the much loved and faithful wife of Jupiter, who was especially revered as the protector of women and goddess of youth and marriage. Strangely, as far as the day of the week is concerned, Monday is said to be good for wealth, Tuesday for health, and Wednesday the best. Saturday, though it is far and away the most popular with most people, is also the unluckiest.

It is a common thing to hear people talk about the wedding ceremony as 'tying the knot', but I wonder how many realize that this is an actual description of what used to happen in a Babylonian wedding, when a thread was taken from the bride's dress and another from the groom's clothes and these were tied together to symbolize their union? And that delightful phrase about 'happy the bride the sun shines on' is a reminder of the old British custom for marriages to be solemnized at the door of the church, and certainly any girl who had to go through this in the rain would be far from happy! Because of such ceremonies, the superstition grew

A chimney sweep wishing good luck to a new bride and continuing in the footsteps of his predecessor who saved the life of a King and, according to superstition, thereby earned the special esteem in which all his kind are now held

up that it was unlucky for there to be an open grave in the churchyard at the time of a wedding, and it was a bad omen for a bridal party to go in the church by one door and out by another, as is done at funerals. At a wedding it is also considered ill-omened if there are an odd number of people present, though I suspect this is again a throwback to earlier times when there was less likelihood of trouble if there was an equal number of relatives and friends from each family present.

Superstition has been busy around the bridal gown, and the importance of the veil and flowers in particular. I can do little better than quote the ancient legend which covers these two items:

There was once a mysterious creature who lived like the wraith of a man or a fallen angel who was especially jealous when a marriage was about to take place. Even if he was not in love with the bride, he was jealous of human happiness in general and did what he could to thwart it, so every precaution was taken and means devised to guard against the malice of this malignant demon or to propitiate the deities. From him the bride hid

Bridesmaids wait to catch the bride's bouquet and hope that by doing so the superstition that they will themselves soon be married comes true!

herself by a veil and received support from her attendant maids. She carried flowers because they were the protectors of humanity and the heralds of peace, for in primitive times they were regarded as symbols of female sex energy.

Of course every bride is encouraged to wear 'something old, something new; something borrowed, something blue', and according to tradition the old item should be her shoes, and the blue part of her bouquet, for her dress should be all white to symbolize innocence and purity. (Green should be avoided at all costs, for it is the colour of the fairies and they are liable to come and steal away someone found wearing it.) Coloured dresses are quite in order for the bridesmaids, although the luckiest colours are blue, pink and gold, with red a most ill-omened colour. A bride who wears a gown her mother or any other forbear wore will be lucky; if she has a new gown she must take no part in its creation. Nor should she look at herself in a mirror in her complete ensemble before her marriage: although the bad luck is usually overcome by leaving off a shoe or glove just in case. This superstition stems from the old mirror belief that part of oneself goes into the reflection, and it would be a bad start to her married life if the bride gave less than her whole self to her new husband.

The bridesmaids are representatives of the 'guards' who once accompanied bridal parties in case they should be attacked by enemies wanting to carry off the bride. Of course the bridesmaid who catches the bride's bouquet can look forward to being married herself within a year, but if any of these attendants should stumble on the way to the altar, I am afraid the saying 'Always a bridesmaid, never a bride' will apply to them. A matron of honour is said to bring particular luck to a bride as she symbolizes the happy state of matrimony.

Humorists have had much fun over the years with the embarrassing situation of a lost wedding ring, but superstition is very grim should either the bride or groom drop the ring during the ceremony. Whoever dropped it will be the first to die; and if it should roll off the altar steps then the marriage is doomed to an early end. The wedding ring strengthens the bond of the engagement ring, and to early man it not only represented a magic circle of union between two people, but also protected the bride against evil spirits. The idea of it being placed on the left hand is because the right is considered superior, and in taking the band on her left hand the woman showed herself subservient to her husband.

The custom of showering the happy couple with confetti as they leave the church is a continuation of a much older tradition from the East of throwing rice to symbolize fertility and the hope that the couple will be blessed with children. In Britain and Europe it used to be customary to strew the pathway from the church doorway with emblems of the bridegroom's profession: wood shavings for a carpenter, small pieces of iron for a blacksmith and so on. Today this custom has been refined to the guard of honour who hold an arch of implements similarly representative over the couple as they leave the church. Tying an old shoe to the couple's car harks back to the old custom of a father throwing one of his daughter's old shoes to her new husband, thereby symbolically transferring the authority he once held over her.

The cake is the focal point of the wedding celebrations and again this is symbolic of fertility and good luck. It was the Chinese who began the custom of giving all friends present at a marriage ceremony a slice of cake and sending pieces to those not able to be present so that all might enjoy good luck. In parts of the world the eating of cake by a man and a woman actually constituted a wedding, but in Britain and Europe a couple ensures good luck and happiness by cutting the first slice together to show they intend to

The very old custom of throwing rice over newly-weds to ensure fertility is demonstrated here after the marriage of the Duke and Duchess of Albany, pictured in *The Graphic*, 1882

Superstition decrees that a newly-wed couple must cut their wedding cake together to ensure good luck and demonstrate they plan to live in harmony together!

live in harmony and share everything and in England for several centuries it was the custom to throw slices of the wedding cake over the bride's head to ensure she bore children. Of course no bride should ever make her own wedding cake or taste it before the appropriate time, and I have heard old country folk say that a bride who keeps by her a piece of wedding cake also retains the love of her husband.

Before the newlyweds withdraw to their married bliss, superstition has two more demands to make of them. First, the husband must avoid bad luck by carrying his bride across the threshold of their new home (or into their hotel room); authorities argue that the origin of this is either to prevent the bride stumbling and thus bringing bad luck on herself, or in deference to the ancient custom that a man had to carry his bride into seclusion if he had stolen her by force or else she might well try to escape. The second belief says simply that whichever of the couple falls asleep first on their wedding night will die first.

A great many of the superstitions that used to surround the topic of sex have disappeared with the march of civilization and scientific progress, but during my researches I have picked up several beliefs which are still occasionally repeated. In Europe, for instance, I heard it maintained that only a virgin could blow a guttering candle back into life or walk through a swarm of bees without being stung. In Britain I was assured that any girl who forgot to put a salt cellar on the table as she laid it was unconsciously indicating she had lost her virginity. As to the sex act itself,

A medieval woodcut of the ancient ceremony of blessing the nuptual bed to ensure fertility for the newly married couple

America proved particularly rich in ideas. There I heard it said that blondes were more eager for sex than brunettes, though redheads beat them both; that hairy men were more vital than those without hair; and that men with large hands and feet and women with generous mouths had larger sex organs than others of their sexes.

The concern with having children is also reflected in superstition, and the wearing of garters has long been thought an aid to fertility, which may well account for them still being considered one of the sexiest items of women's underwear. Throughout Europe it is said that a girl who wears a garter of wheat straw while she makes love will conceive a boy child, while one made of oats will result in a girl. This association of straw and fertility is said to be due to the fact that baby Jesus Christ was laid in a manger and thereby conferred special qualities upon it. Even the weather can play a part in conception, for if it rains while you make love, says an old European belief, you will have a boy, while if it is fine, the child will be a girl.

Even when she is pregnant, superstition is still hovering around the mother-to-be. If she wants the child to be intelligent she should immerse herself in educational books; never look in an empty sack unless she wants the child to go hungry in its life; never steal anything, or her child will grow up to be a criminal; nor should she step over a grave or the child will die prematurely. Some rural Americans have a belief about sexing the child which says a boy baby kicks on the right side of the womb and a girl on the left.

When it comes to the actual birth, it is by no means unusual to hear it said that delivery is made easier if all the locks and doors in the vicinity are opened, and any knots on the mother's clothing untied. Obstetricians would doubtless disagree with the old belief heard around the British coast, that children can only be born as the tide is coming in, and that one born at the ebb is doomed to an unhappy life. I have always found interesting the idea that children born during the hour of midnight can see ghosts, and that the one sure way to make a child 'rise' in life is to carry it up to the top of the house or hospital as soon as possible after its birth. In England there is a belief that any child born through a Caesarian operation will be very intelligent and strong, while the baby whose mother dies in giving birth to it will inherit special healing powers. Any child born with teeth is ill-omened, and you will not bring a baby good luck if it is allowed to see itself in a mirror before it is six months old.

Sunday seems to be by far the best day on which to be born (though Christmas Day is specially favoured, too), and super-

'Carrying the Bride over the Threshold', a painting by Reznicek of another of the very old superstitions associated with the marriage ceremony (1908)

stition has given us a famous rhyme about the attribute of each day:

> Monday's child is fair of face,
> Tuesday's child is full of grace,
> Wednesday's child is full of woe,
> Thursday's child has far to go,
> Friday's child is loving and giving,
> Saturday's child works hard for a living,
> But the child that is born on the Sabbath Day
> Is blithe and bonny, good and gay.

A British superstition says you can ensure your baby's future by presenting it with specific gifts as soon as it is old enough to understand their significance: bread (food), salt (intelligence), an egg (friendship), a coin (wealth) and some matches (to light its way). In America I was told people tried to determine what the future held for a young child by placing in front of it some money, a pack of cards and a Bible. If he reached for the first, the child would be financially secure, the second, it would be a gambler, but the third ensured a happy, healthy and prosperous future. On both sides of the Atlantic it is recorded that a child who is allowed to urinate in the fireplace will quickly become clean and dry, and, though it may be scant consolation when it is bawling late at night, a child that cries a great deal will also live a long while.

And so to baptism, which superstition insists is important if a child is to thrive and grow strong. This ceremony drives off the evil spirits which are said to lie in wait for an unbaptized child, though in several European countries a form of protection suggested for a baby is always to cover it in at least one item of its father's clothes. The naming of children has always been important in old beliefs, and no baby should ever be named after another which has died in infancy and is in any way related. And, of course, anyone who names their child after someone who is famous is consciously or not trying to attract some of that person's luck to their offspring.

It has always been considered lucky for a child to cry at its christening, for this is a sign that the evil spirits which would plague their later life have been driven out by the Holy Water. The idea of giving silver cups and spoons and even small gold items to the baby after this ceremony is said to have its origin in the offerings of the Three Kings to Jesus after his birth in the stable in Bethlehem. And as to the party which should be thrown afterwards for relatives and friends, this should be as lavish and well supplied with drinks as possible. Superstition is particularly insistent on the liquid refreshment to ensure the child's good fortune – doubtless this is the origin of the expression 'wetting the baby's head'.

CALLERS at our home often look very surprised when I answer their knock on the door.

Having heard me whistling along the hall they expect to see a man.

I have always whistled, though my mother did her best to stop me when I was young.

She used to say " A whistling woman and a crowing hen would frighten the devil out of his den."
—Grace Cooke, Oldham, Lancs.

Another superstition still at work – from *The Sunday People*, 7 January 1979

William Hogarth's charming engraving of a Christening ceremony

CHAPTER 7

THE TRADITIONS OF SPECIAL DAYS

The crowning of the May
Queen – a very ancient
custom, surrounded by
superstition, that is still
practised in parts of the
British Isles. This turn of the
century drawing is by
Randolph Caldecott

'Happy New Year!' –
welcoming each new year is a
popular custom all over the
world, and one which is
steeped in old superstitions

'New-Year's Eve in
Edinburgh', a picture by
W.B. Murray from *The
Illustrated London News*,
January 1876

Superstition plays an important part in many of our annual high
days and holidays, although it is perhaps only fair to say that for
most people a lot of the activities indulged in at these times have
lost their original meanings. Take Midsummer, for instance,
which was once one of the most important days of the calendar
when men and women celebrated the summer solstice with a
variety of rituals and special customs. Today it is a popular night
for a big dance, but the only customs which have survived are those
undertaken, perhaps with some embarrassment, by young country
girls looking for lovers. This said, the superstitions behind special
days of the year, whether widely observed or not, make fascinating
reading and explain why we do certain things on these days
probably quite unconscious of their significance. I propose to
consider them in calendar order, beginning at the New Year.

The most famous custom at New Year is, of course, 'first
footing', in accordance with the old belief which appears to have
originated in Scotland, 'the first foot over the threshold decides the
luck of the year'. At the first stroke of the new year, a dark-haired
man (a noted exception to the almost invariable rule of superstition
that anything dark is ill-omened) should be admitted through the
front door bearing a lump of coal, apparently to ensure that the
household will not be short of fuel during the year. With the
passage of time, many people have forgotten that originally the
'first footer' carried a coin and some bread as well as the coal, to
symbolize the three things most desired for any family: money,
food and warmth. Tradition is also specific that the luck-bringer
should not be a fair-haired man or woman unless the household
wish to court misfortune. As New Year's Day represents the
rebirth of the year, there is also supposed to be a kind of wonder-
working magic in the air which has given rise to the practice of
making resolutions because they, too, symbolize a new beginning
for man himself.

Superstition also says that everything which happens during
these crucial first hours of the year sets the pattern for the twelve
months to come and it is therefore a good idea to have full
cupboards, pockets and stomachs and not to let the fire go out! If
you fancy indulging in a little fortune-telling, there is a tradition
noted on both sides of the Atlantic that if you take a Bible on New
Year's Day, open it at random and place your finger on the page
without first looking, the passage you have indicated will give you a
clue to what the year holds in store. (The Bible also features in a
number of similar superstitions where omens for the future can be
divined by opening it in a certain way, but this is the only one I
have heard of still being used.) There is something to be said, too,

John Keats celebrated St Agnes' Eve – when superstition says young girls can hope to dream of their future lovers – in his famous poem. This illustration for the poem is by Robert Anning Bell (1910)

An early, hand-made Valentine card of the kind superstition says will be most effective in winning a loved one's heart

for the final New Year's belief that you can ensure yourself a year of good luck by being the last one to finish any bottle of drink.

The evening of 20 January, known as St Agnes' Eve, has been popular for generations with young girls in many rural areas of Britain, for on this night it is said they can see visions of their future husbands. The tradition seems to have developed from the fact that St Agnes, the patroness of virgins, was martyred on this night in the year 306 by the Emperor Diocletian, and certainly the custom has been recorded by such distinguished authorities as Ben Jonson and John Aubrey, who wrote in his *Miscellanies* (1696) instructing young girls that on this eve, 'you should take a row of pins and pull out every one, one after another, saying a Pater Noster, sticking a pin in your sleeve if you will dream of him you shall marry.' John Keats wote a poem, 'The Eve of St Agnes', which says:

They told her how, upon St Agnes' Eve,
Young virgins might have visions of delight,
And soft adorings from their loves receive
Upon the honeyed middle of the night,
If ceremonies due they did aright;
As supperless to bed they must retire,
And couch supine their beauties, lily white;
Nor look behind, nor sideways, but require
Of heaven with upwards eyes for all that they desire.

One of the most widely used love spells for this night involves knot-tying which has always been symbolic of forming unions. Before going to bed the girl must twist her left garter about her right stocking and repeat the lines:

This knot I knit
To know the thing I know not yet,
That I may see
The man that shall my husband be.

In parts of Scotland and Ireland it is still the custom for unmarried girls to make a 'dumb cake' on St Agnes' Eve. This consists of flour, water, eggs and salt and has to be made and baked in absolute silence. Then it should be eaten just before going to sleep and it is said to induce a vision of the maker's husband-to-be.

St Valentine's Day, which falls on 14 February, is much better known for young love, although the original customs have become swamped by commercial exploitation. Today millions of cards and mementoes are produced for admirers to send to those they admire; the original intention was that the cards should be handwritten and drawn and the verses composed by the sender. The early Greeks and Romans both observed 14 February as a special day for their respective goddesses, Hera and Juno, who represented women and marriage, but the day was made famous by the Christian Church who linked it with St Valentine, a young priest who defied the edict of the Emperor Claudius that soldiers should not be allowed to marry as it made them poor fighters. St Valentine ignored this ruling to conduct the weddings of a number of young soldiers, and was executed for his pains on 14 February, 269, thereafter becoming the patron saint of lovers. The custom of sending cards did not begin until the Middle Ages. Since then superstition has been busy and one of the most universal customs is wearing St Valentine's flower, a yellow crocus, on this day to ensure luck in love. Incidentally, if you see a yellow bird of any kind on the 14th it is a good omen.

Among many young girls in English country districts there is a belief that to see a hen and cock together early on St Valentine's Day is a sign they will be married during the year, while the number of animals seen first thing in the morning will indicate how many months before this happens. The first kind of bird seen is also said to be a guide to what sort of man he will be: a sparrow indicating a countryman, a robin for a sailor, a blackbird for a clergyman, and, perhaps most desirable of all, a goldfinch for a wealthy man! I must remind you that it is very unlucky to sign a Valentine card; if you do the omens are against you ever marrying the person concerned.

The next notable date on the calendar is Shrove Tuesday, the day which was set aside for confession before the beginning of Lent. Its more popular name is Pancake Tuesday, and these pancakes are the last remnants of the huge feasts that used to be put

One of the famous pancake races held on Shrove Tuesday in the village of Olney in Buckinghamshire. It is very lucky to be able to eat a piece of any of the pancakes that survive the race intact!

on before the Lenten abstinence. With the passage of time it has come to be considered lucky to eat pancakes on this day, although they must be consumed before eight o'clock in the evening. The relevance of eight o'clock would seem to be that in feudal times this was the curfew hour, when all lights and fires must be put out. In any event, a great many people still observe this particular super-stition, and the pancake races held throughout the country are always a constant delight to the press and television.

When a Leap Year occurs and we get that extra day of 29 February, we are urged to lose no time in beginning any important undertaking for it is sure of success. This day gives young women a chance to propose marriage to reluctant lovers without fear of misfortune. A Scottish relative told me not so long ago that there was an important adjunct to this that the girl must observe: she had to wear a scarlet flannel petticoat, visible below her dress. This, he assured me, was where the term 'scarlet woman' had originated.

April Fool's Day has escaped the attention of superstition, except that it is unlucky to play any trick after midday. The origin of the custom of playing practical jokes on people on this day comes from France and dates from the sixteenth century when the existing calendar was changed, moving the first day of the year back from 25 March to 1 January. People were annoyed over this interference with a popular festival, and in retaliation numbers of citizens began sending local officials on false errands and then taunting them with the fact that it was April the first. So when you are next enjoying yourself playing a prank on someone on April Fool's Day remember you are doing it because your ancestors objected to having New Year's Day in the middle of winter instead of at the opening of spring which would seem to be a much more natural time.

Easter is perhaps only exceeded by Christmas in the number of ancient superstitions that still cluster about it. Long before its Christian significance, Eastertide was a festival associated with the spring equinox and sun worship. Hot cross buns owe their importance to both for although it is now customary to eat them on Good Friday spiced bread was originally central to pagan spring festivals and eaten in the hope it would bring a year of good fortune. The Ancient Greeks stamped each piece with a horned symbol as an offering to the goddess, Astarte. Following the development of Christianity, buns were made representative of the unleavened bread which Christ ate with his disciples in the upper room, the cross representing the sign he had made over each piece before it was eaten. Over the years it has come to be considered lucky to eat at least one of these buns on Good Friday, and there are still

people who say they can cure certain stomach complaints, and to hang one in a building will protect it from bad luck or fire. However, while it may be lucky to bake on Good Friday (nothing, apparently, will go mouldy), it is not a time for gardening, nor for washing, in particular. This last idea grew up because of the washerwoman who is supposed to have waved a wet garment in Christ's face as he was led to Calvary and to have been reproached: 'Cursed be everyone who hereafter shall wash on this day.'

The idea that it is lucky to put on new clothes at Easter is also much older than Christianity and again is symbolic of renewal. It was the early Christians, though, who made the practice widespread, and in their case a change of clothes was no doubt a necessity after the long period of Lent when they had fasted, gone unwashed and sprinkled themselves with ashes in penance. They put on new garments for the rejoicing of the resurrection on Easter Sunday, and from this developed the belief that it was unlucky not to have at least one new item of clothing to wear on this day. A curious reversal has occurred over an associated claim that anyone who ignored this custom was ill-starred and would find themselves the target of bird droppings; apparently birds knew of the importance of the day and took exception to anyone who failed to show the proper respect. Curiously, the tradition has changed with the passing of time and today it is said to be actually *lucky* to be hit by these droppings when wearing something new on Easter Sunday!

Easter eggs, which are given to children on Easter Sunday, are also part of a tradition that goes back to the times of the Ancient Egyptians, as well as the Romans; both saw the egg as a symbol of rebirth and made family presents of them. Since those times the egg has become a universally accepted good luck charm, and one of the luckiest things a person can do is to open one with a double yolk on Easter Sunday. Although few people believe eating one on this day will lead to a happy and healthy year, it is still felt to be courting fortune if coloured eggs are given to loved ones, especially to children. Those painted or dyed red are most auspicious. This idea appears to have developed from the days when the first Christians adopted the egg as an emblem of the resurrection of Christ and when coloured red served as a reminder of the blood he shed upon the cross. Sadly, today many parents seem to have dropped this custom and instead give their offspring chocolate eggs, which I have yet to hear enjoy any kind of luck-bringing qualities.

The first of May, May Day, is now regaining a little of its former importance since being declared a public holiday. Once it marked the start of the Celtic New Year, and was also celebrated as the

Though hot cross buns are traditionally eaten on Good Friday, the origin of the custom goes back to pagan times, and several other superstitions are also associated with the buns

The Germans celebrate May Day in many villages by selecting a young virgin and then covering her with flowers and fruit to ensure a good harvest

The famous ceremony of crowning a May Queen

Roman festival of Flora, in honour of the goddess of fruit and flowers. Then there were sacrifices and special rituals in order to ensure the gods sent fertility and a good harvest. The Christian Church adapted the older customs to make the day a popular spring festival, but Oliver Cromwell effectively put a stop to everything during his period of government. Nowadays little of the original atmosphere remains, although it is still possible to find villages where there are dances round the Maypole (a remnant of the fertility rites) and countryfolk who will leave bouquets of flowers on the doorsteps of neighbours they like, and bunches of weeds or thorns on those who have offended them. In places, too, there are girls who believe their complexions will be improved by washing their faces in dew first thing on May morning, and the crowning of the May Queen as a custom is still observed in some rural districts. May Day is also a very popular day for displays of Morris dancing, and superstition holds that such dances encourage corn crops and vegetables to grow. However, the most persistent belief about this day – and indeed the whole of the month – is that it is a most ill-omened time in which to get married. As a very popular saying insists, 'Marry in May – you'll rue the day!' This goes back to the earliest times when May was considered the most

Morris dancing is another popular custom on May Day and superstition says that these dances encourage local crops to grow

important and busiest month for planting and sowing crops and no hands could afford to be idle. As a result such time-consuming events as marriages were forbidden and from this eventually grew the idea that May was an unlucky time to wed. In America, I am told, it is still the custom on May Eve for young girls to leave their handkerchiefs on bushes in the hope that on the morning after they will see in the dew the initials of the one they are to marry.

As I mentioned at the beginning of this chapter, Midsummer has been stripped of most of its old superstitions, and instead we content ourselves with open air dances and barbecues if the weather is fine. In country districts, though, there is still a delightful belief that if a girl slips an ash leaf between her breasts and repeats the following words before going out for the evening she will see her future husband (which if she is going to a dance is just possible, I suppose!):

The even ash leaf in my bosom
The first I meet shall be my husband.

Perhaps the most publicized event of midsummer is the gathering of the modern order of Druids at Stonehenge. These people, who claim to be continuing a ritual dating back to antiquity, assemble around the altar stone at daybreak and there conduct a ceremony of sun worship.

The current revival of the ancient cult of witchcraft, or Wicca as it is known, has seen the re-emergence of some ancient customs on this night, for Midsummer is one of the four most important evenings in the witchcraft calendar. The night is known as Lammas which celebrates the union of men and women and usually includes a ritual marriage in which a young man and woman 'jump the broomstick' in the cult's time-honoured way. Magic is also worked to ensure health for the members of the coven, as a group of witches is called, and a rich harvest in the autumn. (Incidentally the other important dates in the witchcraft year are Candlemas, 1 February; May Eve, 30 April, and Halloween, 31 October.) These ceremonies aside, it is still possible to find country villages where fires are lit on Midsummer Eve in accordance with an old belief that they will drive off the evil spirits who might spoil the harvest.

A curious belief persists that it is lucky to eat goose on Michaelmas Day, 29 September, although I have been unable to find any explanation other than the old rhyme which decrees:

Who so eats goose on Michaelmas Day,
Shall never lack money his debts to pay.

And if you examine the bones of a roasted goose after you have enjoyed the meal, the colour of them will serve as a weather omen: if they are brown, the following winter will be mild, whereas if they are white or bluish then it is going to be hard.

With the onset of winter we come to one of the best known days of the year, Halloween, 31 October, the remnant of a pagan feast of the dead. Innumerable superstitions once surrounded this day, which is now marked by night-time games for children such as 'Trick or Treat', and special masked parties for adults. From the very earliest times, this day was said to mark the moment when the supernatural forces symbolizing cold and death returned to earth, and it was necessary to combat them in some way so that man might survive the darkness and dangers of the coming months. Fires were burned which were supposed to drive away the spirits so that they could not injure man or his livestock through the winter. The night is also supposed to be one when witches and warlocks are abroad, riding on broomsticks to their great Sabbats, and indeed modern practitioners of *Wicca* hold special gatherings on this night which they call *Samhain*.

A Victorian magic lantern slide showing the use of a turnip head to frighten two young girls on Halloween

Legacy of Dickens's snowy childhood

By Stewart Tendler

Now that copies of Bing Crosby's record have been returned to the BBC library for another year it can be disclosed that a white Christmas is something of a myth. According to one of Britain's leading climatologists, the childhood of Charles Dickens is to blame.

Records at the Meteorological Office in London show that there have been only two genuine white Christmases this century. In 1906, 1917, 1927, 1956 and 1968 snow fell on Christmas Eve or Boxing Day but only in 1938 and 1970 did snow fall " deep and crisp and even " on Christmas Day.

Mr Hubert Lamb, head of the climatic research unit at East Anglia University, says his researches into weather records show that in the first eight years of Dickens's life there was a white Christmas every year with either snow or a white hoar frost. "The idea of a white Christmas possibly owes a good deal to Charles Dickens and *A Christmas Carol*", Mr Lamb says.

Mr Lamb adds: "The idea of a white Christmas is fairly mythical. Christmas Day and the days either side have a rather good sunshine record. The most characteristic picture is of a rather quiet, sunny period between more disturbed winter weather.

White Christmases are just a myth according to the statistics discussed in this report from *The Times*, 3 January 1978

Because it was believed apples and nuts had special powers to drive off witches and evil spirits they featured in several old Halloween love divination customs which have persisted in many places to this day. For example, if a single girl stands in front of a mirror during the course of the evening and eats an apple, then it is claimed the face of the man she is to marry will appear in the glass, and if a couple place two nuts side by side in the fire, the way they react will predict their future. If the nuts burn steadily to ashes without any untoward movement, the couple can expect a long and happy married life; but should the nuts burst and fly apart when touched by the flames, then the omens are bad. Of course, even if we do not partake in such superstitious nonsense, we unconsciously honour the old traditions by roasting chestnuts on the fire or taking part in the game of 'apple ducking', trying to catch apples floating in a bowl of water with our teeth. (The fact that there were omens to be read from the size of apple you caught is virtually forgotten now; once, the bigger the apple you landed the greater your fortune would be, while if you could catch nothing, then you were doomed to poverty.) Most of these customs have become associated with Halloween, but they probably originated with the Romans, who held a festival at the end of October each year to honour Pomona, the goddess of fruits, which in those times chiefly meant nuts and apples.

What with the witches and warlocks supposed to be abroad, not to mention young boys with pumpkins hollowed out and illuminated with candles to form gruesome faces, it takes a brave girl indeed to undertake the other Halloween love divination I came across, for she must creep out into the garden at midnight and pluck twelve sage leaves: and as she does this the shadowy figure of her husband-to-be is supposed to approach her from the other side of the garden.

Young Scots girls are said to have a better chance to learn about their future husbands on St Andrew's Night, 30 November, and according to Martin Luther (in his *Letters, c.* 1530) 'on the coming of the feast of St Andrew, the young maidens in this country strip themselves naked and in order to learn what sort of husband they shall have, they recite a prayer'. Another mating superstition which seems to persist is that if a girl sits alone in her bedroom until midnight, then at the moment the clock strikes twelve flings open the door, she will get a fleeting vision of the man who is to be her husband.

We have now reached the end of the year, and perhaps the greatest, certainly most popular, of all special occasions: Christmas.

An old engraving of Father Christmas filling stockings with gifts. His origins are said to lie in superstition . . .

Although most of the Christmas stories can be traced back to Christian origins, there are some which are clearly older and probably associated with Yule, the ancient end-of-the-year feast of the dead. The mistletoe, for instance, which is such a delightful highlight of the decorations, was revered by the ancient Greeks as sacred, yet superstition has it that the reason why it is lucky to be kissed under it is that the plant once offended the old gods, who thereafter condemned it to have to look on while pretty girls were being kissed! Holly derived its name from the word 'holy', and is a suitable decoration for three reasons: first its evergreen leaves represent eternal life; secondly, the red berries are a reminder of the crucifixion of Jesus Christ; thirdly, its prickles are an ideal deterrent to all evil spirits. A good display of holly, says superstition, will ensure a happy and lucky Christmas.

Food, of course, plays an important part in the celebrations, and it is as well to remember that the Christmas pudding must always be stirred in a clockwise direction, that is 'the way of the sun' or bad luck will follow and the pudding will be spoiled into the bargain. Don't forget to add the small coins or charms that will bring good fortune to those who find them. The wishbone from the turkey or chicken, always highly prized by whoever receives it, has come to be looked on as lucky because of its resemblance to the horseshoe. The belief that you can have a happy year by eating mince pies is also still very widespread, although superstition is more insistent that you will only get the good luck if you eat *one pie per day* from Christmas Day to Twelfth Night, each pie consumed giving you a month of good luck. The origin of this belief seems to date back to Roman times, although a more popular explanation is that the first mince pies were not round and topped with pastry as today, but oblong and open at the top, thereby symbolizing the manger in which Jesus was born.

The most charming of all Christmas superstitions concerns the legend of Father Christmas and his visit on Christmas Eve to fill children's stockings. According to an old legend, St Nicholas, patron saint of Christmas, visited the home of three very poor girls one Christmas Eve, and when he saw how miserable their lives were, threw a handful of coins down the chimney. The money did not fall into the fireplace, but into some stockings which the girls had left to dry before the embers: imagine their surprise when they discovered the gifts in the morning. From this humble beginning grew the belief that Father Christmas visits homes by way of the chimney and leaves his presents in stockings.

The custom of decorating a Christmas tree again goes back to pagan worship, when the tree gods were honoured by dressing up

The customs and traditions of Christmas – an evocative engraving of the Victorian Yuletide from *The Lady's Newspaper* of 27 December 1851

Europe's biggest Christmas tree in London beside the Houses of Parliament. According to superstition a Christmas tree in the home will ensure a year of light, warmth and good fortune for the whole family

certain trees with ribbons and coloured objects. The lights and candles we put on the tree are of Christian origin, though, for they are supposed to signify the lights that lit the Holy Family's way to Bethlehem. A well-decorated Christmas tree is said to ensure a year of light, warmth and good fortune for all the household. The actual weather on Christmas Day is also significant in a couple of old beliefs: if the sun shines there will be a fine harvest later in the year, while snow signifies there will be more deaths than usual in the neighbourhood.

Holy Innocents' Day, which follows on 28 December, and is sometimes known as Childermas, is widely believed to be the unluckiest day of the year. The origin here is clearly the slaughter of the innocent children by King Herod, and over the years there has been a persistent refusal among many people to work or begin any new project on this day. There is even a story that the coronation of Edward IV was fixed for the Sunday after Christmas Day until it was suddenly realized that it was Childermas and the arrangements were hurriedly switched to a more suitable date.

And so, finally, to Twelfth Night, which, though it falls in the New Year on 6 January, puts the old year in order and ensures your luck for the new one. Once upon a time there were many superstitions attached to this day (which was originally Christmas Day) but nowadays we only pay regard to the belief that *all* decorations (and that includes Christmas cards) must be taken down or the family will be blighted with bad luck. It is apparently imperative that the evergreen decorations should be burnt and not just thrown away, and the Christmas tree must be either replanted or destroyed at the same time. If for any reason you are unable to do this, wait until 2 February (Candlemas) when you will have one last chance to avert a year of mishap and unhappiness!

Superstition says that all Christmas decorations must come down on Twelfth Night to avoid bad luck – and that particularly includes evergreen decorations such as the mistletoe! A picture by R. Anning Bell (1910)

CHAPTER 8

SUPERSTITION AT WORK AND LEISURE

The ceremony of laying a foundation stone or placing a coin in the foundations of a new building derives from the custom of earlier times when human or animal sacrifices were made by burying them alive in the foundations. This was done to appease the particular earth spirit on whose territory the building was to be constructed

Perhaps because there is an element of luck required in quite a number of professions, and certainly most sports, it is only to be expected that superstition is widely found in these areas of our lives. In a variety of such activities, those taking part depend to a great extent on forces beyond their control to achieve success, or else to overcome a deeply rooted sense of insecurity, real or imagined, and so consciously or not will turn to forms of luck-bringing 'magic' for assistance. It is interesting to note, too, that while the profession or sport may be comparatively modern, the origins of the superstitions appertaining to it may be of very ancient origin indeed.

Take, for instance, the general belief among many professions that it is ill-omened to brush waste material out of any building or factory for fear of 'brushing away' the chance of future jobs: the waste should be swept into piles and then removed in a bucket or container. In the dressmaking industry I have heard it reported that to 'dust the table with a piece of paper is to dust away the work'. In both these instances, the origin of the belief goes back to the very earliest times when man did not like sweeping anything from his dwelling place for fear of pushing out the good spirits who guarded him and his family and allowing the evil ones who dwelt outside to enter in their place. Even the 'rag trade', the mass production end of sewing and dressmaking, has attracted its fair share of superstitions which cling doggedly to it. It is said to be unlucky to lose a thimble, and seamstresses should never lend each other needles as this will 'prick' their friendship. It is lucky, of course, to see a pin and pick it up, although you should never pick up a pair of scissors you have dropped, but let someone else do it for you unless you want to attract bad luck. The fortune, good or bad, attracted to all such implements has evolved from the ancient belief in iron being a sacred metal.

The rapid changes in industrial and commercial life have naturally driven away many of the superstitions attached to the older professions such as carpentry, masonry, milling, baking, weaving and so on, for where once these were the pursuits of men working on their own, now they have either been absorbed, dissolved or taken over entirely by the infernal machine! But in their place has appeared something perhaps more fearful still, as Eric Maple has so well expressed it in *Superstition and the Super-stitious*:

Even in the vast factory complex there are islands of mystery as frightening to certain individuals as any tabooed shrine of a pagan faith. One accepts, of course, that some individuals will be more accident-prone than others and for this there is indeed actuarial support. But how is one

SHIVER OUR TIMBERS— HE'S A JINX!

By KEN YATES

LIKE the gun slingers of the old West, Arnie Ward can clear a saloon by just walking through the door.

Not that he's a mean hombre. And he certainly doesn't tote a gun.

But he does upset the fishing folk at Scarborough, Yorks.

They say undertaker Arnie is the unluckiest man they know.

They call him a sea jinx and blame him for storms, sea mists and various other calamities.

Last week Arnie's reputation landed him in trouble with Mr. Walter Bird, landlord of the Lord Nelson on the foreshore. Arnie was asked to leave the pub.

Said Mr. Bird: " When Arnie walked in my fishermen customers all dodged out of the back door. I couldn't let Arnie upset them, so I asked him if he would go somewhere else.

" He took it all in good part and went off. He doesn't think he brings bad luck."

Another seafront landlord, Mr. James Haig, of the Lancaster Hotel, said: " The fishermen tell incredible hard-luck stories after seeing Arnie.

" I'm afraid I'd have to turn him away if he called for a drink."

Fishing boat owner Harry Sheader explained how Arnie, 59, had earned his strange reputation. He said: "When he is about everything goes wrong. But he doesn't seem to realise it."

Overboard

Another fishing boat owner, Albert Fishburn said: "We have lost crab pots, we have had engine trouble, cables have snapped, and we have had poor catches.

" And a man once fell overboard when he stepped back to talk to Arnie on the dockside."

But Arnie, of Southmere Drive, Great Horton Road, Bradford, takes it all in his stride.

He said with a grin: "I will be back to see them in the Lord Nelson when I visit Scarborough again later this summer.

"Fishermen are very superstitious. They believe anything. I pull their legs. The tales just grow.

"They blame me for everything that goes wrong. I can empty a pub full of fishermen quicker than anyone. But I am really the fishermen's friend".

Their friend? Joked Harry Sheader: "Never trust an undertaker. He'll let you down in the end."

Superstition at work in more ways than one – a newspaper report from *The Sunday Mirror*, 2 June 1974

to regard the sincere belief among many industrial workers that an individual has become a jinx solely because he has a record of accident-proneness in consequence of which men will be reluctant to work with him? There are 'jinx' machines, too, from power looms to machine tools, which, like the traditional dog with a bad name, constantly live up to their ill-omened reputations for creating trouble or accidents, and which workmen will strenuously avoid using. Here in a completely modern setting is expressed one of our most primitive superstitions, the belief that an inanimate object can acquire not only a form of life of its own but almost human characteristics.

This said, we do still find a greater number of superstitions at work in the traditional occupations. It is still very widespread for trades-people of all kinds to spit on the first money they take in the morning in the hope it will give them a good day's takings. The reason for this is an old belief dating back to at least Roman times that spittle has the magic power to encourage good influences and drive away bad ones. In country districts many shopkeepers believe they will not have a good day unless they keep the first coin paid to them and do not give it in change. And it is ill-omened to turn a calendar to a new date before it arrives, or inadvertently date any bill or sales ticket a day or more ahead.

The chimneysweep, of course, has a special place in superstition, and no bride can wish for a better start in married life than to leave the church after her wedding and be confronted by one of

Steeplejacks have a superstitious belief that they can protect themselves from falling by twisting their braces, thereby creating the 'knot' that represents safety

these men. He may well have been specially placed there, but the good luck will be just the same once she has given him a kiss. It is believed that the sweep earned his lucky reputation during the eighteenth century when one of his kind saved the life of an English King, probably one of the Georges: the alert sweep is said to have caught the reins of a frightened horse running away with the monarch on its back. The man disappeared into the crowd before the King had time to thank him, and, knowing it would be impossible to recognize the fellow again beneath his soot and grime, he gave instructions that all sweeps were thereafter to be treated with honour and respect just in case they should be this man. Also as a result of this it is said that to meet and shake hands with a sweep before any important event will ensure good luck, and it is on record that before the Duke of Edinburgh married the Queen (then Princess Elizabeth) in 1947, he slipped out of his apartment to do this with a sweep who just happened to be passing by!

Unlike the chimneysweep, the window-cleaner feels himself menaced by superstition, particularly as his trade is at the mercy of the weather and he runs the risk of danger every time he mounts his ladder. One of the most popular of all beliefs is the idea that it is unlucky to walk under a ladder, the reason for which I explained in the first chapter. Window-cleaners say that a ladder with an odd number of rungs is lucky and that they should always erect them in the same way; it is very ill-omened to reach for anything through the rungs.

The steeplejack, who similarly deals in heights, has a nice superstition that he can protect himself against a fall by tying together or twisting his braces, thereby creating the 'knot' that traditionally represents security. Steeplejacks also have a custom of 'topping out' a newly erected building or steeple by placing some kind of decoration on the top (a piece of laurel, perhaps, or a ribbon in a lucky colour like blue) to ward off evil spirits and protect all those who go inside.

In the building trade, any construction where a workman is killed or dies is said to be ill-omened. The custom of laying a cornerstone or placing a coin in the foundations of new buildings is regarded now as a pleasant little ceremony, but it is actually the remnant of a most unsavoury business. In earlier times man looked on each piece of land as being the particular preserve of an earth spirit, and the only way to avoid offending this being when placing a construction on his territory was to make a sacrifice. Initially these sacrifices were children, buried alive in the foundations or walls. Later animals and precious objects took their place, until now our only reminder of the gruesome superstition is the laying of a foundation stone. Builders also believe it is tempting fate to write about any construction until it is actually finished, and quote the examples of the King's Bridge in Melbourne and the Frejus Dam, both of which were the subject of premature articles and promptly collapsed almost before the cement was dry.

Another set of folk who take their lives in their hands up in the sky, aeroplane pilots, have their own particular superstitions. A large number of them wear lucky charms of one sort or another, and there are several instances of pilots who claimed their rabbit's foot charms enabled them to land disabled aircraft safely. No pilot would use the word 'crash' before taking off, and there is a general aversion against having red flowers on board. Some American pilots have been known to have the safety belts in empty seats crossed before take-off, and to empty all their pockets on landing as a symbolic offering to the gods for a safe flight.

Among the more down-to-earth occupations, superstition has

The pilot of this plane that crashed close to an electric railway line near Southend, Essex, in 1960, but miraculously without death or injury to anyone, was carrying a lucky rabbit's foot charm in his pocket at the time!

also been busy. Some farmers still take notice of many of the old beliefs we have discussed in earlier sections about crops and livestock, but it is interesting to learn that a number of them believe produce of all kinds grows best when sown from north to south. Actually, this is quite logical, for the seeds are more exposed to the sun when sown this way instead of from east to west. In Europe I have heard farmers say it is unlucky to express too much admiration for any livestock, particularly those being sold or exhibited, for this will affect their chances. Where doctors are concerned, we know that much early medicine was surrounded by superstition, but progress has inevitably swept all that away. However, there are still those who think it is unlucky to call out a doctor on a Friday – for they will not get better – and that the first person seen by a doctor in a new surgery is bound to be cured. Nurses, too, cannot escape superstition, and if they knock over a chair in the ward it is a sign there will soon be a new patient arriving (more than likely, I would have thought!), and to put blankets over a chair while making a bed is an omen of death. This belief seems to have originated from the old custom of wrapping the dead in woollen blankets before putting them in their coffins. Superstition has even influenced the colouring of pills, red and pink being much used because of their association with blood and blooming health, and black avoided because of its connection with death.

According to recent reports, a growing army of superstitions have been developing around motor cars and – like homes – it is said they all fall into the category of being lucky or unlucky. A number of salesmen have reported extreme difficulty in selling cars in which someone has died, while there are other vehicles which seem jinxed, and no matter what care is taken in maintaining them, they constantly go wrong or are involved in accidents. Several such vehicles are said to have had the number 13 or been purchased on Friday the 13th. (Friday has gained its unenviable reputation because it was the day on which Adam and Eve were thrown out of Eden, when Christ was crucified, and the traditional day for the execution of criminals. Thirteen, of course, has been an unhappy number because of the thirteen who celebrated the Last Supper.) It is ill-omened to boast of trouble-free motoring, but lucky to stay with the same make of car which has proved reliable for you. Perhaps, though, the most widely held belief about the car is that as soon as you clean it, rain will start to fall: which is just the latest variation on the very old idea that any action you perform invites the gods of nature to imitate you – in this case by 'washing' the car with rain.

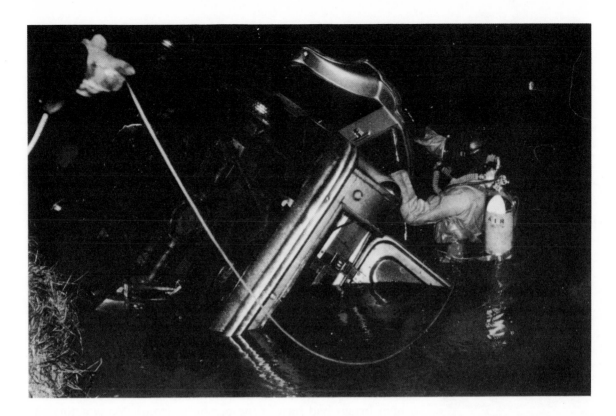

The end of an ill-omened car. Vehicle BAE 13 was bought on a Friday the thirteenth and finally crashed into a Hertfordshire river on a Friday the 13th in 1963

Miners, because they take part in what is still dangerous work despite all its mechanization, have not been able to throw off all their old superstitions. For example, it is still said to be unlucky to whistle underground – you might annoy the subterranean spirits who would cause a subsidence – and that it is a bad omen for a cat to be allowed anywhere near the workings. Miners on their way to the pit do not like to see a cross-eyed person – a remnant of the old idea that such people had the 'evil eye' – and only a brave-hearted man would go down if a dove or robin was seen near the pit-shaft, for this is a sure sign of a disaster. It is further said to be unlucky for a miner to return home for anything he may have forgotten; if he must do so, he should knock on the window three times before going in for it.

Many more professions are similarly under the influence of a superstition or two, but without doubt the one group of people most affected by it are actors and actresses, whose whole careers are often said to be 'in the lap of the gods'. The very fact that the success or failure of a play depends on how the actors perform and how the audience reacts to them makes the theatre a rich breeding ground for all manner of omens and superstitions. Theatres themselves are often considered lucky or unlucky, and it is not unusual for one that has had a string of failures or suffered accidents on or off stage to have its name changed. A black cat has always been a lucky animal in any theatre (the Haymarket Theatre in London used to keep one there permanently), but it is a bad sign

An illustration of the three witches from Shakespeare's *Macbeth*, a play beset by ill omens. The witches' song in particular should never be sung anywhere except on the stage or bad luck will strike the production

if it runs across the stage during a performance. The number thirteen is avoided on seats or dressing-rooms in many theatres, and in quite a number of places it is said that if the first person to purchase a ticket for a new production is old then it will have a long run; if they are young it will not survive beyond a few weeks. Real flowers should never be used in a production: they are more likely to be upset by an actor than artificial ones, and consequently spoil the performance (real food, drink and jewellery are also frowned on); nor should peacock tail feathers adorn any costume as the 'evil eye' will adversely affect the other actors. The colours yellow and green are avoided because they show up badly under the lights (they were also Satan's colours in the old Mystery Plays) and most actors think three candles on stage or in a dressing-room will lead to a quarrel. Any actress who knits either on or off stage is likely to 'tie-up' or entangle the production.

In the dressing room, it is said to be unlucky to whistle (it 'whistles up' failure for the play) or to look over another actor's shoulder into his mirror (another remnant of the 'evil eye' tradition which brings bad luck to the person in front). Many actors and actresses believe good luck resides in their make-up boxes (to lose one is certainly a terrible catastrophe) and they should never be tidy, but cluttered, and if a lucky rabbit's foot is kept there it can serve both to ensure good fortune and to apply rouge.

Chorus girls believe if they spill powder on the floor it should be danced over quickly before being wiped up. During rehearsals it is said to be a bad sign if there is a perfect run-through, and the last or 'tag' line should not be spoken until opening night. (The fear here is that by 'completing' the play it is laid open to the hostile reaction of the gods of chance.) Naturally, to stumble on entering the stage is unlucky, or to catch any item of clothing on the scenery, similarly to have a prop such as a door fail to work. No performer should ever be wished 'Good luck' – quite the opposite, in fact, and one of the most popular wishes is 'Break a leg'! Actually to fall during a performance is a good sign, for it is said to win the sympathy of the audience, but if an actor misses a cue he will keep on doing so throughout the performance unless he retraces his steps and begins again. One could indeed go on almost endlessly with the personal fetishes that different actors have, but each has usually evolved from some past success which the person concerned hopes will be repeated.

Throughout the acting profession, Shakespeare's *Macbeth* is considered a very unlucky play and one likely to be beset by problems when produced. Its lines should never be spoken off-stage, nor should the famous witches' song be sung anywhere

Enrico Caruso, perhaps the most superstitious of all actors. He is dressed here for his role of Alfred in *La Traviata*

except on the stage; it is, in fact, this song which is given as the reason for the play being considered unlucky, for it is claimed that it actually has the power to work real evil. And there is no denying that there have been a string of accidents happen in various theatres throughout the world where the play has been staged. For instance there were two riots, one in New York and one in London, when *Macbeth* was put on in the early part of the nineteenth century. Incidentally, two pantomimes *Robin Hood* and *The Babes in the Wood* are widely believed to be unlucky, while *Cinderella* has the reputation of being very fortunate.

Musicians, too, have their superstitions, and it is well known that both Chopin and Rossini believed in the power of the number thirteen, as did Richard Wagner, whose life was literally governed by it. He was born in 1813 and his name contained thirteen letters; his famous opera *Tannhauser* was first performed on 13 March 1845, and he died on 13 February 1883. Mozart was apparently obsessed by omens and when he was commissioned to compose his *Requiem* he declared, 'I am certain that I am writing a requiem for my own funeral.' He felt convinced it would be his last work, and that was exactly what it proved to be. As a general rule musicians believe that when they make a mistake playing a piece they should stop and begin all over again, and that it is bad luck to recommence a piece of music they have been practising if they have been interrupted for any length of time. They should try a few bars of another piece before going back to the original.

There are even several ill-omened songs including 'I dreamt I dwelt in marble walls' and Tosti's 'Goodbye' which are said to bring misfortune if sung outside their normal context, being suggestive of death and separation respectively. Another song in this category is 'Gloomy Sunday' used as the theme tune in Orson Welles's film *The Third Man*. Apparently when it was first performed in Budapest in the 1940s it proved so melancholy that it caused a spate of suicides and its performance had to be banned by the Hungarian government. Perhaps the most superstitious of all entertainers was the great opera star, Enrico Caruso, who aside from the more usual beliefs was afraid of hunchbacks and would not travel on a Friday or wear a new suit on that day. He put everything untoward that happened to him down to some superstition or other and even claimed that a series of minor accidents that happened to him on one occasion were the result of the 'evil eye' being put on him by an interviewer.

Just as all entertainers need more than a little luck in their gamble with success or failure, so the gambler courts Lady Luck, whether playing for fun or profit. Indeed gamblers are every bit as

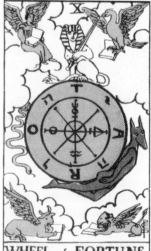

WHEEL of FORTUNE.

THE LOVERS.

DEATH.

superstitious a group of people as those who make their livelihood on the stage. The impulse to gamble is as old as history, and nowhere is the feeling that the magic of luck can be summoned up more evident than in card playing, cards themselves often being known as 'The Devil's picture books'. (They probably got this reputation from their predecessors, the Tarot cards of the fortune-teller.) Many of the superstitions relating to them seem to have evolved from their origins in France in 1392. Devised as an entertainment for King Charles VI, the four suits represented the four classes of French society: Hearts the clergy, Spades – being like the points of spears – the military, Clubs the emblem of farmers and peasants, and Diamonds for the merchants and bankers.

When playing cards, it is important not to cut them crosswise as this is symbolic of cutting one's luck, and many a player will attempt to 'cross out' his opponent's luck by placing matchsticks in the form of a cross on the table or in an ashtray. The old belief that it is unlucky to play on any surface other than green baize is quite sound, for on a polished table the cards in your hand might be reflected so that your opponent can see them. If a player is having bad luck, it is said he can change this by walking around the table, changing his seat, or asking for a new set of cards. Bridge players believe they should circle the table three times, always from left to right, thereby going in the direction of the sun and hoping that great orb will shine his blessing on them. At the same time, the action also 'encircles' the bad luck. It is a bad omen to drop a card during a game of Bridge, and if it is a black ace the player should withdraw immediately. Also never let a dog in the room while playing poker, never hum or sing as you are sure to lose, and if playing for money, stack all your winnings in neat piles. To 'play a hunch' has an interesting origin, for hunchbacks are supposed to have luck-bringing qualities if touched before a game. As Francis Bacon, the philosopher, explained: 'Deformed persons are commonly evil by nature, for as nature has done ill by them, so they by nature are beings devoid of natural affection.' Therefore by touching such an 'evil object' one is given assistance in warding off the forces of evil and bad luck.

Gamblers who play roulette place great reliance on lucky charms such as pieces of bone, rabbit's feet, locks of hair, four-leaf clovers, tiny horseshoes and coins with holes in the middle. The idea that a pretty girl by your side brings luck is just as popular. It is ill-omened to lend money to another gambler – and the belief still seems to persist that anyone playing the tables for the first time cannot lose. I have heard it said that this 'beginner's luck' is based

-Gary Player, the top golfer, is a strong believer in omens and said recently, 'Superstition can be a positive force for better golf.'

on that very ancient custom of holding anything new in awe, in this case a new player.

In America, playing dice, or 'crap shooting' as it is known, is seemingly the most popular form of gambling, although it is not widely appreciated that the expression originated from the French. There it was the practice of young boys to play dice crouched in corners away from the disapproving eyes of their parents. They had the appearance of toads, and so the game earned the name of *crapaud* after these creatures, and in turn the Americans shortened it to 'crap'. There are many superstitions attached to dice playing, but the most popular seem to be that good luck can be attracted by rubbing the dice on a redheaded person, blowing on them, snapping the fingers (to drive away evil spirits), or touching them against the genitals or breasts to endow them with procreative power.

'The sport of kings', horse-racing, is full of superstitions, and many punters even after the most meticulous study of form will still follow the oddest hunch. Many believe it is lucky to meet a cross-eyed woman on race day, to use a pin which has come from a wedding dress in making their selection, and to pick a jockey wearing their favourite colours. By far the majority are personal and based on some past success. Jockeys, too, are a notoriously superstitious group of people. Many of them have lucky riding crops which they believe it is ill-omened to drop before a race, just as they never stand their riding boots on the floor for this is symbolic of being unhorsed. It is also reported that jockeys think it is unlucky not to be spoken to by their real names before a race; and they, like owners and punters, believe that if you kiss a horse after it has won a race this ensures its luck for the future!

Golf superstitions seem to be more prevalent in Britain than America, perhaps because the game has been played here longer, although I have heard players from both sides of the Atlantic say they believe it brings bad luck to approach a tee from the front, clean a ball when you are playing well, or to change your mind about a club once you have selected one for a shot. I suspect psychology is more at work than superstition in the claim that a golfer who is 'two up and five to play' at the thirteenth hole will never win the game: by keeping a grip on himself and his game, there is really no reason why he should let such a lead slip away. Indeed, golfers seem to scorn the idea that thirteen is in any way ill-omened, and many of the top professionals actually carry thirteen clubs on a round. A ball bearing the number three, five or seven is said to be lucky, but I am not sure that the belief 'He who wins the first hole will lose the match' is given much credence although it is

Opposite: Three of the most influential cards in the Tarot pack

Superstition lets second boat into first place

By John Nicholls

Superstition played a part in allowing David Tabb and Mark Lewis to win the practice race of the Hornet class world championship, at Thorpe Bay yesterday. They were lying second to Kenneth Herve and Keith McIlwain as they approached the finishing line after a slow race

Yachting is a sport much influenced by superstition and as this cutting from *The Times* of 15 August 1977 shows, the idea of not tempting the fates by winning too often is still firmly entrenched!

still widely repeated.

American baseball players are a group almost obsessed with omens. No player who sees a cross-eyed woman in the stands, for instance, will make a hit, but if he catches sight of a red-head fortune is going to smile on him. Hairpins have always been collected by baseball players for they are said to be symbolic of base hits (the great Leo Durocher had an enormous collection of them at one time), and as each bat is believed to 'contain' just so many singles, doubles, triples and home runs, a player gives away some of his own luck if he loans one to a team mate. It brings good luck to spit on a baseball glove, and when a player goes out to bat he should leave his glove with the fingers facing towards his own team's dugout. A dog crossing the field of play is an ill-omen for the team at bat, although it has always been a good sign to see empty beer barrels before going to the plate, though the reason for this is quite unknown!

In tennis it is unlucky to use a ball that has been returned after a fault, and even if you have a large enough hand to do so, never hold three balls while serving. Cricketers are beset by personal superstitions, but among those generally held is that it is lucky to see a black cat when going out to bat, but unlucky accidentally to put your pads on the wrong legs. Any cricketer who stumbles when he leaves the pavilion is in for a poor spell with the ball.

Football, of course, gives some of the clearest demonstrations of superstition at work. Supporters with their decorations, rattles and endless chants are all trying to conjure up the 'magic' necessary for their team to win, while the team itself often adopts a small boy as mascot in the hope he will bring them luck. Many players have personal idiosyncrasies about the way they put their boots on, the order in which they go on to the field, and certain activities they carry out before the kick-off. The often heard claim that certain players dislike being watched by their wives or girl friends is probably an unconscious throwback to the old witchcraft belief that a woman could put the 'evil eye' on somebody merely by looking at them.

Some boxers also share the fear of the 'evil eye' being put on them, and a number of champions have had their own personal good luck charms, like the old-timer, Bob Fitzsimmons, who always insisted on a horseshoe being nailed up in his training camp, and Ezzard Charles who never went into the ring without his 'lucky robe'. In general, it is unlucky for a fighter to see a hat lying on his couch before a bout or to wear new boots for the first time in an important contest. And the reason for the challenger having to enter the ring before the champion in any title bout is because long ago a champion insisted that it was unlucky to be first, and when he won his superstition became a precedent.

Angling as a sport has attracted an enormous following, and because of the element of luck required to complement the angler's skill, has acquired its own particular superstitions, not a few of which are similar to those observed by sea fishermen, which we shall discuss in the next chapter. The river angler does not like to be asked how many fish he has caught, nor would he put his keep net into the water until he has landed his first fish, for both are tempting Providence. It is unlucky to change rods during fishing or substitute one float for another: by doing so anglers believe they run the risk of changing their luck; and any bait which is not spat upon before being put on the hook is unlikely to catch a fish. There is a strange belief in Scotland that an angler who is not getting a bite can remedy the situation by throwing another fisherman in and then hauling him out; the fish are so impressed by this, apparently, that they will then imitate the performance. Perhaps, though, you would be better following the American maxim summed up in these words, 'Fish East means fish bite least; fish West fish bite best'.

Yachtsmen and weekend sailors are also often influenced by the superstitions of those who go to sea for a living. It is not uncommon for crews to throw a small coin into the sea before setting out, as a gift to the gods for a trouble-free voyage. Many a yacht has a gold coin placed under its mast to bring luck to the vessel, and only the most foolhardy owner would paint his craft green. When it comes to racing, there is plenty of evidence that many yachtsmen believe it is better to be second in a practice race or preliminary heat, so as not to challenge the fates by believing your luck will allow you to win the same event twice.

And at this point we may conveniently head for the open seas . . .

Sean Connery of James Bond fame has good reason to believe in the power of superstition. While playing roulette at the St Vincent casino he backed his favourite number 17 three times and it came up on each occasion, winning him $30,000!

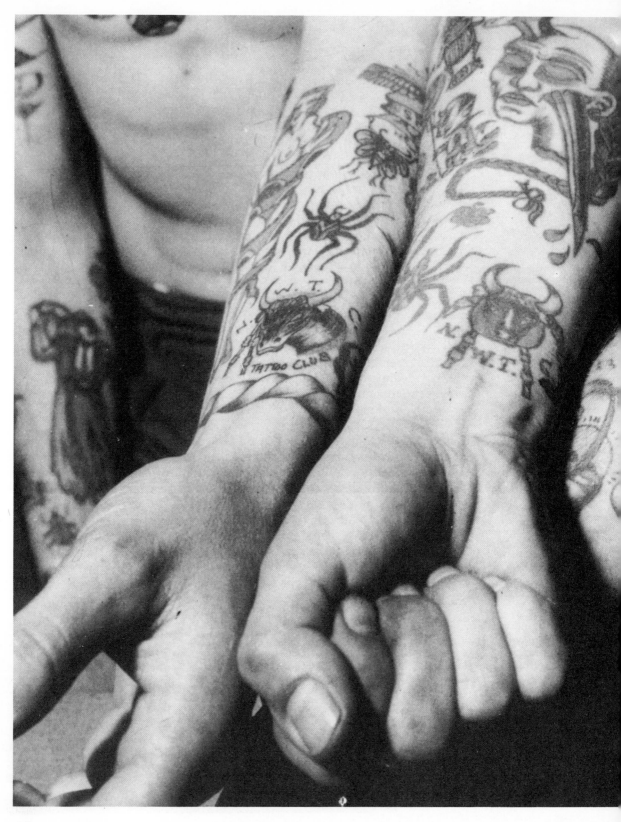

CHAPTER 9

PERIL AT SEA

Since ancient times sailors
have adorned themselves
with tattoos to ward off evil

Since the earliest times ships
have often been painted with
an eye to both protect the
vessel and 'see' the way
ahead

Not so many years ago, when a ship sailed from port there was
really no telling whether it or its crew would ever return. Dependent on their own skill and the guidance of the sun, moon and stars,
at the mercy of wind and weather, and without any of the modern
inventions of communication, sailors not surprisingly looked for,
and believed in, any omens that might come their way. James
Fenimore Cooper has expressed the situation most succinctly in
his book, *The Water Witch* (1834):

There is a majesty in the might of the great deep that has a tendency to
keep open the avenues of the dependent credulity which more or less
besets the mind of every man. The confusion between things which are
explicable and things which are not gradually brings the mind of the
mariner to a state in which any exciting and unnatural sentiment is
welcome.

Of course today sea voyages are no longer a journey into the
unknown, which explains why many of the old superstitions
appear to have passed into oblivion. But, as any hardened sailor
will tell you, in the right circumstances, in time of danger or peril,
they have a very real habit of re-emerging in the thoughts of
mariners. These same men would not think twice about calling
someone who brings bad luck to a voyage a 'Jonah', or quietly
paying tribute to that malignant sea spirit Davy Jones, who has
power over the ocean itself and commits all those who defy the
customs of the sea to his famous locker. These are good reason, I
think, for examining all such beliefs in some detail here.

It is not, for instance, difficult to understand why for centuries it
was believed to be unlucky to watch a ship disappearing from sight
over the horizon, or to point at it as it went. You were reluctant to
trust the vessel to the care of the gods of the deep and might incur
their anger to the extent that they prevented its safe return. The
idea of painting eyes on the prow of a boat also goes back to
antiquity, for the very earliest men to venture on the seas believed
their craft to be 'blind' and needed these eyes to see their way. In
certain countries, too (China is one), sailors cut holes in their sails
to prevent the evil spirits which haunt the sea getting caught up in
them and harming the ship. And, of course, belief in mermaids, sea
serpents and phantom ships was widespread among men of the sea,
and still is among some of them today.

Bad weather is the thing the seaman fears most and it has
become surrounded by superstition, as Thomas Gibbons says in
Boxing the Compass (1901): 'There is but a plank between a sailor
and eternity and perhaps the occasional realisation of the fact may
have had something to do with the broad grain of superstition at
one time undoubtedly lurking in his nature.' To whistle on board a

A seventeenth-century engraving of the kind of sea monster that was believed to dwell in the depths of the great oceans

ship is to risk 'whistling up' the wind, although sailors have been known to use this belief to their own advantage when becalmed; however, it must not be overdone or the storm gods will punish the ship and the whistler. It is an interesting fact, by the way, that the name often given to British public houses, 'The Pig and Whistle', originated through this superstition, for not only did the sailor feel confident that he could whistle once safely back on land, but he also knew that the use of the word 'pig' was said to be unlucky when at sea; if the creature had to be mentioned at all it should be called a hog or sow.

In some ports along the British coast I have been told it is still maintained that if a seaman's wife combs her hair or cuts her nails while her husband is afloat she may cause a gale at sea; I suspect, though, that this is a variation on the old tradition that witches collect up hair and nail parings to use in their evil spells: and witches, of course, were past-masters at stirring up storms at sea.

As much as possible is done to protect a boat from the elements right from the moment it is first put into the water. The ceremony of launching a new vessel by breaking a bottle of champagne across its bows is straight from the annals of superstition. In the infancy of sail men believed it was necessary to propitiate the gods of the deep with a sacrifice before committing it to the waves, and these first tributes took the form of human or animal blood spread on the bow. The Greeks and Romans altered this tradition by splashing red wine over their boats and giving them female names as

Phantom ships crewed by the dead were said to haunt the seas, as illustrated in this fifteenth-century Flemish engraving

Beautiful figureheads on the prows of sailing ships are said by superstition to be harbingers of good luck and a protection against danger while at sea

symbolic 'brides' to Poseidon and Neptune, the gods of the sea. It is from them that we gain the tradition of referring to a ship as 'she' and placing beautiful female figureheads on the prows of sailing craft. Naked women are also supposed to be luck-bringers and able to protect a ship from danger. By custom, the person performing the launching should be a member of royalty, but this seems to have fallen into disuse in recent years, though it is still considered unlucky for the future of the ship if the bottle of champagne does not break at the first attempt.

Naturally enough no ship should be numbered thirteen, and it is said to be unlucky for a vessel to have a name ending with the letter 'a'. I have been unable to discover the reason for this belief, but the ill-fated *Lusitania* is quoted as the perfect example of the superstition at work. It is also said to be very unlucky to change the name of a ship, and it used to be the custom to destroy by fire any craft that had gained a sinister reputation. No shipowner ever wants to purchase a vessel with a history of disaster, as bad luck is said to follow such 'jinx' ships. Friday is claimed to be a day on which no new ship should be launched or voyage begun. The belief seems to have stemmed from a seemingly endless number of doomed craft which set out on this day, and which are commemorated in a rhyme recalled by seamen in ports all over the world:

On a Friday she was launched
On a Friday she set sail,
On a Friday met a storm,
And was lost in a gale.

There have apparently been numerous attempts to try and disprove this particular superstition, and there is a story that during the First World War, the British Admiralty, in its desperate need for new warships, arranged for one to start construction on a Friday. By coincidence, it became ready for launching on a Friday, and the Sea Lords decided to lay the old belief finally to rest by sending the ship on her first voyage on a Friday, under the command of a Captain Friday, too. She set sail – and was never heard of again! This said, the shipping records of any major port will show Friday to be as busy a day as any other in the week.

A superstition just as old as this one, but with an element of truth in it, is that rats will leave a sinking ship. The fact is these creatures hate to be wet, and if a vessel is beginning to leak – the first sign of disaster – they will go looking for new quarters. Cats are lucky creatures to have on board, particularly all-black ones – and they also act as a weather omen, for when they are particularly lively, sailors say they have 'the wind in their tails' and are giving warning that a storm is brewing.

Any ship with a name ending in the letter 'a' is said to be ill-fated – and the sinking of the *Lusitania* on 7 May 1915 is quoted as the best example of the superstition at work

Birds naturally figure a great deal in the lore of the sea, and there is perhaps no more famous one in this context than the albatross. It is said to be extremely unlucky to kill one for they play a special part in determining the weather and are believed to contain the souls of drowned sailors. These beliefs are certainly very old, but for many people the source is that marvellous poem *The Rime of the Ancient Mariner* by Samuel Taylor Coleridge (1798) in which the sailor who has killed the albatross bemoans his fate in these words:

And I had done a hellish thing,
And it would work 'em woe.
For all averred, I had killed the bird
That made the breeze to blow.

Seamen read many omens from the changes in the elements and the activities of birds and fishes that appear near their vessels. Seagulls should never be killed or misfortune will befall the ship; three of them flying overhead close together is a death omen

An actual case of this ill-luck happening occurred in 1959 when an albatross was being transported from the Antarctic to a zoo in Germany and died shortly after the ship had left port. Thereafter the vessel ran into a succession of storms, engine troubles and other misfortunes which so upset the crew that they went on strike. Eventually the vessel limped into Liverpool quite unable to go on – and the captain blamed the whole thing on the dead albatross.

PERIL AT SEA

The seagull is another bird that should not be killed or misfortune will befall a ship, and the sight of three of them flying overhead close together is a death omen. A seagull that brushes against the window of a house is indicating that someone who lives there and is currently at sea is in danger; while the sight of seagulls far inland has always been regarded as an indication of storms on the way. The petrel is an unlucky bird and because its appearance was supposed to be the first indication of bad weather, it became known as the 'storm petrel'.

Dolphins, those lovely creatures who now delight crowds in marinas and are believed by scientists to be one of the most intelligent species after man, have always been highly regarded by sailors. According to very ancient traditions, it was said that if a school of dolphins was seen playing round a ship in fine weather, then the crew should take note that a terrible storm was on the way. On the other hand if they showed up near a vessel while bad weather was raging, then they were clearly indicating that a let-up was imminent. Much study has gone into this particular belief, and scientists such as Thomas Pennant, writing in his *British Zoology* (1924), are convinced that here is a superstition that stands the test of actual observation. Porpoises give similar warnings by their presence near a ship.

Whales are also lucky creatures, and it may be a comfort to those who are fighting so hard to conserve the whale population that nothing good will come to those who kill them. The sight of a whale close to shore or in an area where they are not usually seen is an omen of trouble to come. The shark has long been credited by sailors with the ability to 'scent' death and it is claimed that if a group of three or more of them follow a ship persistently then there is going to be a death on board. (In fact, they are most likely to be following in the hope of scavenging the scraps of waste food thrown overboard.)

Since the very earliest days of sail it has been considered that to have a dead body on board ship will lead to disaster. The origin of this is a legend that the soul, once it has left the body, becomes afraid that it will not receive Christian burial and therefore sets about wrecking the ship so that the corpse will at least descend to the sea bed. Should this not be done, and the body be carried on to some distant port, it may in the meantime be occupied by an evil spirit who will prevent it rising again on Judgement Day. Fascinating though this argument is, it seems more likely that even years ago seamen were aware what a health hazard a corpse presented, and wanted it disposed of as soon as possible – hence the practice of burial at sea. The equally curious idea that a dead body

Sailors have long held to the superstition that tattoos will protect them from evil spirits and misfortune. This selection of elaborate designs should certainly do the trick!

on board slows down the progress of a ship seems to have disappeared years ago, and as the debunking of this is so intriguing I think it worth mentioning here. I found the reference in an old book entitled *A Helpe to Memory and Discourse* (1630) which refers to the superstition in the form of a question and answer:

Question: Whether doth a dead Body in a shippe cause the shippe to sayle slower and if it doe, what is thought to be the reason thereof? Answer: The shippe is as insensible of the living as of the dead; and as the living make it goe the faster, so the dead make it not goe the slower, for the dead are no Rhemoras to alter the course of her passage, though some there be that think soe and that by a kind of mournful sympathy.

Ancient superstition is behind the practice of flying flags on a ship (apart from the practical use they have of conveying messages) for originally ships were garlanded with flowers believed to be most pleasing to the gods. The widespread practice among sailors of decorating themselves with tattoos is rooted in superstition and the belief from primitive times that such markings protect the wearer from evil spirits and misfortune. For this very reason many of the symbols they wear are of good luck charms like crosses, hearts, flowers and so on. It was once a custom of wives and sweethearts to give heart-shaped pin-cushions stuck with pins to sailors to bring them luck and avert the storms caused by demons.

Of considerable antiquity, too, is the ceremony of 'Crossing the Line'. Today, on cruise liners, it has become a boisterous, comic event, with Neptune and his Court lathering, shaving and ducking anyone who has not crossed the Equator before, but originally it was an act of worship which could even include a sacrifice to show honour to the sea. Formerly the ducking of an apprentice to the sea was done when the ship passed well-known capes or islands, and he was actually tipped overboard at the end of a length of rope rather than into a swimming pool, so that he was forcibly reminded of these important landmarks as well as being 'sacrificially' offered to the gods of the sea. Later, as scientific navigation took the place of coastal voyages by guesswork and landmarks, the 'line' or Equator was chosen for the observance of the custom.

Sailors have apparently always considered it ill-omened to have a priest or minister on board a ship, and on merchantmen and cargo ships women are believed to be unlucky. Pregnant women, though, are not (nor children for that matter) and in this lies the clue to the superstition: for doubtless a solitary woman among a group of men at sea for any length of time would be bound to raise passions and, inevitably, trouble. Seamen also allegedly dread a new moon on Saturday, or a full moon on Sunday. One can explain the first, because Friday was once the day dedicated to love, which itself was supposed to increase with the increase of the moon. So a new moon falling on a Saturday would have undoubtedly been preceded by a very dissipated Friday evening, almost certainly resulting in a very unseaworthy crew. But quite what harm would occur as a result of a full moon on a Sunday, which has only been a sacred day in comparatively recent times, is difficult to see.

Only a sailor who was not superstitious would think of leaving his ship left foot first, and most hope that the first group of people they see on land make up an odd number. (Perhaps in deference to this superstition, the Navy requires all salutes to be given in odd numbers.) Not so long ago it was considered unlucky to meet a sailor fresh from the sea, and to avoid bad luck it was necessary to pinch him! I believe this may have originated from the early days of sail when a man went to sea and might well not be heard of for a year or more. Consequently no one could be sure if he was dead or alive, and as most people were afraid of ghosts the only way to be sure the returned mariner was real was to pinch him and see if he made a noise. (More than one authority has suggested this custom may also be the origin of the expression, 'Pinch me in case I'm dreaming', which people use when something remarkable happens.) Nowadays we look at sailors in quite a different light, and any young girl who touches a sailor's collar should be in for some good luck. The seamen, for their part, believe that they can ensure a safe voyage by touching their wife or girlfriend's pudenda – a custom which has become known as 'touching the bun'.

As I said at the beginning of this chapter, many of these superstitions are scorned by modern sailors, but fishermen, particularly

deep sea fishermen putting out from the smaller ports of the world, are not so quick to dismiss them, and indeed have added quite a considerable number of their own. Perhaps in the light of the sailor's belief that their womenfolk can safeguard their voyages, it is a surprise to find that fishermen do not like to meet a woman when on their way to their boats. European fishermen are particularly nervous of seeing a nun, while in Britain any woman they do not know is ill-omened, especially if she should be barefoot. At the bottom of this belief is a fear that to see a woman will lead to either no catch or a very small one indeed.

The wearing of St Christopher medallions seems to be very popular among fishermen, but for generations stones with holes through the middle – known as 'Holy flints' – were believed to be most effective at warding off evil influences and the seagoers either wore them on strings around their necks or hung them up in their boats. Here is obviously another form of the symbolism of the womb, which, through fecundity, begets luck. Children collecting sea-shells along the seashore are actually following a tradition fisherfolk used to observe, for necklaces of these shells were once believed to offer protection against drowning while at sea. The horseshoe is also regarded as a lucky charm, and it is still the custom among some Scottish fishermen to have a small piece of rowan tree nailed to the mast. There are American fishermen who believe it is unlucky not to have a mascot of some kind on board, usually preferring a small animal. By and large, though, fishermen do not like animals on any ship, and even the mention of pigs, hares and rabbits is considered unlucky. If a man inadvertently mentions one of these creatures he and his crew members must grab hold of the nearest iron implement and shout, 'Cold iron!'

The fisherman needs good weather, of course, and this can so easily be influenced by things which happen. For instance, it is not good for him to be spoken to when on his way to his boat, nor to be wished 'good luck', and he must always remember to carry his sea boots under his arm and not over his shoulder. I have myself heard fishermen at Cape Cod on the Massachusetts coast repeat the following lines when consulting the weather conditions before setting out to sea:

Comes the rain before the wind,
Then your topsails you must wind;
Comes the wind before the rain,
Haul your topsails up again.

Of course, there are not many fishing boats under sail these days, but old fishermen maintain that the omens should still not be

Fishermen all over the world still cling to a number of old superstitions that they observe in the hope of bringing them luck and a good haul when they put to sea

The caul, or thin membrane which envelopes the foetus in the womb, is believed by sea folk to be able to protect them from drowning if carried to sea. For this reason they have been bought and sold in many ports

ignored. There are those who believe it is unlucky to repair and use again a vessel that has been wrecked at sea and later washed up on the shore. However, in many coastal districts it is said to be very ill-omened to break up an old boat that has become unseaworthy. The rotting, partly submerged hulks of old wooden boats that can be found around the less populated areas of the British Isles and along parts of the coast of Europe bear witness to the application of this superstition. Because the sea has borne the vessel throughout its 'life', the belief claims, so should it be allowed to claim it when its usefulness is over.

Although I only ever heard the superstition mentioned once in a rather vague way, I must mention a belief which apparently was once very widespread, that a fisherman could be sure of a good catch if he beat his wife before going off to sea. Charles Platt explains the idea more fully in his book, *Popular Superstitions* (1925):

Of course it must not be done on purpose – it must be a normal quarrel, not a forced one, and it is extremely fortunate if blood is drawn. Obviously the woman would have to be naked, or very lightly clad indeed – possibly her night-clothes, as fishing boats often set out at night – or else a normal marital whipping would not draw blood from the body of a strapping, well-built woman. That word strapping, by the way, strongly suggests that healthy men and women were supposed to be those brought up on the strap.

Another curious idea, but easier to understand, is that boy babies are born at high tide and girls at low, while somebody who is dying but survives a change in the tide will not die until the tide has turned. Here we have yet another example of the fate of man being somehow linked to the rhythm of his environment, something that can be seen as a very prevalent factor in superstition. Charles Dickens certainly knew of this belief and mentions it in *David Copperfield* when Mr Peggoty says to the dying Barkis, 'People can't die along the coast except when the tide's pretty nigh out'; and another character remarks, 'He's going out with the tide – he's going out with the tide.'

Fish themselves can provide the fishermen with a number of omens. Many a herring fisherman will tell you that it is a good idea to look at the first catch of the season, for if the fish you examine is a female then you can look forward to a run of good hauls. Scottish fishermen believe the haddock is a lucky fish, and there is a legend that the black spots on each side of the head near the gills were made by Christ's fingers when he divided a haddock among the five thousand he was feeding. In parts of the world it is believed that large shoals of fish swimming near the water's surface are the

According to superstition bathing in the nude will bring you good luck. It is a belief that Brigitte Bardot for one has observed for some years!

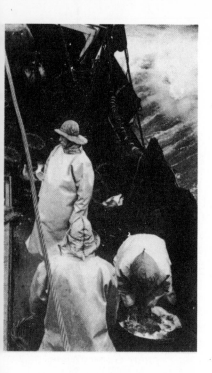

Some fishermen still believe in the old superstition that you should examine a fish picked at random from the first haul of the season and if it proves to be a female then you can look forward to a run of good catches

sign of a storm brewing, which may in part account for the belief that fish bite well three days before a storm. On the shore itself, sea-urchins thrusting themselves into the mud or trying to cover themselves with sand are also said to presage a storm. I have heard a story that fish somehow 'know' when a murder or tragedy has taken place and will desert a stretch of coast where such a thing has happened. The people of Normandy in France say this is exactly what happened following the defeat of Napoleon at the Battle of Waterloo in 1815.

All around the North Sea there still seems to be a belief that to strike a glass accidentally is an omen that a sailor somewhere is going to be drowned: it seems the ringing tone the glass makes has become identified with the tolling of the death bell which has always been sounded when news of a shipwreck reached land. In this same area of the world there are captains of fishing vessels who might be inclined not to put to sea that day if they found a hatch the wrong way up, for this is said to be symbolic of the boat itself turning upside-down. The very least they would do would be to offer a quick prayer to St Nicholas, the patron saint of sailors, who saved himself and the crew on board a ship sailing to the Holy Land, when it was struck by a storm; it is for this reason that we find many churches dedicated to him close to the sea.

Finally, in this chapter, a few words about bathing in the sea, and the awful prospect of drowning if you are not careful. According to superstition it has always been unlucky to get your feet wet before your head, as the feet are considered inferior. (In actual fact, it is not a bad idea to wet your face and head before plunging in as this can overcome the risk of a headache brought on by blood pressure. And as we know that such a thing could easily lead to cramp and the risk of drowning, superstition here is certainly advocating sound good sense.) In the context of bathing I also picked up a charming belief that it was lucky unexpectedly to come across someone bathing in the nude. Quite why, I have not been able to determine, but if the person should be a beautiful girl there can be no disputing the luck!

One of the most persistent of all beliefs about drowning is that a person in this dilemma sees their whole life flash by them in an instant; while another equally strong claim is that a drowning person will surface at least three times before finally sinking. A belief that mercifully seems to have disappeared is that it is *unlucky* to save someone from drowning: once it was felt such a person was marked by the gods of the deep and if you deprived them of their rights they would surely punish you in the fullness of time. In the past, when every voyage to sea was a journey into the unknown,

An ill-omened ship. No shipowner would buy the *Bywell Castle* after it collided with the pleasure steamer, *The Princess Alice*, on the River Thames in September 1878, resulting in the death of 630 people. It had to be broken up for scrap

and few sailors could swim, such an attitude was no doubt understandable. And to end on a rather bizarre note: a recent report from America based on police and coastguard statistics seems to confirm a superstition that goes back to Roman times and beyond: that drowned men almost always float on their stomachs while women are found face upwards.

CHAPTER 10

OMENS OF DEATH

A rare photograph of Aleister
Crowley, nick-named the
'Great Beast', who mixed
magic and superstition to
create an occult order which
attempted to solve the
mysteries of life and death

Your action replay at the exit

NEW YORK: Accident victims DO see their lives flash before them just before they die.

Interviews with 100 survivors of near-death situations reveal that the emphasis is on pleasant experiences.

Most of the people entered a state of dream-like serenity that helped produce vivid pictures from the past.

One of the oldest superstitions seemingly proved after all these years – a report from *The Sunday People*, 25 March 1976

OMENS OF DEATH

When I was in the Deep South of America a short while ago, I was told of a superstition still very widely regarded by Negroes that if a sick person suddenly calls out the name of someone who is dead it is a sure sign that his or her own death is not far away. I have to confess that when I heard this I could not suppress a shudder, despite the fact that it was a steamy day and I was taking breakfast in one of the most fashionable restaurants in New Orleans. The belief is certainly very old and more than one Negro I subsequently spoke to said it was known in Africa from the earliest times. If one analyses the superstition it is possible to find a sound psychological base to it, for it is a well established fact that when the mind becomes feeble with approaching death it has a tendency to return to the past, and the mentioning of someone from this past is a clear indication of what is happening.

In America, too, I heard the belief expressed that the last name a dying person mentions will be the next to die, which again is possible if the person referred to is a close relative such as a husband or wife. By way of contrast, on a trip in Europe I heard it said that if someone is unintentionally reported to have died before they in fact do so, they will gain an extra ten years of life.

Death omens, of all the groups we have considered in this book, tend to have more of an effect on even the most unsuperstitious people, and I suppose the very fact that death is so inevitable for all of us, and so mysterious, has much to do with this. 'The fear of death is more to be dreaded than death itself', wrote Publius Syrus, the Greek scholar, shortly after the advent of the first century, and he was expressing something that was as true then as it is today. Though there was and is no denying every life must end at some time, the very fact opens up speculation as to what happens thereafter. Could there be an after-life, and if so, in what form does man as we understand him in this life continue to exist?

Charles J.S. Thompson in his book, *The Hand of Destiny* (1932), has defined why this area of superstition has become so important to mankind:

Many curious superstitions and customs have been associated with the final stages of life from remote times, for the mystery attached to death has ever evoked a certain sense of fear and dread among human beings. The idea underlying such omens, signs and portents, appears to have been derived from the early belief, that the gods in some manner or other, at times, revealed to man an indication of future happenings. This knowledge to a certain degree was at first confined to soothsayers and magicians, but as time went on, it became popular property and traces of it are still to be found in the folk-lore of the people. Prognostications or omens of approaching death or fatalities are common to all races, for it can be readily understood, that the mind when racked by anxiety through the

Superstition is much concerned with death, and the great artist Hans Holbein, who was himself a superstitious man, drew on some of the beliefs current in his time for his marvellous series of illustrations, 'The Dance of Death', of which this is one example

presence of sickness or impending death, becomes over-sensitive to sounds and sights.

Already in earlier parts of this survey I have given examples of death casting his shadow in the form of omens, but here I should like to note some more specific instances which I have found to be repeated from place to place. Perhaps the most commonplace of these is that an involuntary shudder is caused by someone walking over your future grave. Plants and trees blooming out of season are widely held to indicate a death in the owner's family, and this particularly applies to apple and pear trees; to dream of a tree being uprooted in the garden carries a similar warning. And if a large number of flowers come into bloom at any time other than their usual one, then superstition says the next winter will be a hard one and there will be more deaths than usual. Several animals are credited with being able to 'see' death coming, or to sense its presence, the dog being foremost among these. Hence the claim that a dog howling outside a house at night is an omen that someone inside is going to die; a dog making this kind of noise at any time when someone lies sick has the same meaning, and if it proves impossible to quieten the animal or drive it off, people say this makes death doubly assured.

A horse which neighs continually through the night is said to be a similar omen, and in some parts of Britain a like interpretation is put on an ox or cow breaking into a garden. There is a saying in Scotland that when anyone is dangerously ill and unlikely to recover 'The black ox has trampled upon him'. In Wales particularly, any indications of disturbance of the soil near a dairy which could have been made by a mole is said to be an indication that the woman of the family will die in the coming year.

Many different kinds of birds are believed to indicate death if they fly close to a house, or actually come into it, but a raven, crow, cock and owl seem to carry the strongest warning. Julius Caesar, for one, is said to have heard an owl hooting during the day before his assassination.

That curious creature the death watch beetle actually got its name as a result of an old superstition that when it was heard scratching in the wood of a building it was indicating a death to come. (In fact the insect makes the noise when communicating with another beetle and bores through wood quite silently.) Any knocking sound in the walls of a house where someone is ill is believed to be a death omen in most parts of Britain, while in Ireland if the noise is heard on three consecutive nights then someone in the house is to die whether there is sickness or not. The explanation of these noises is that they are made by Death to

The life of a clock is said by superstition to be bound up with that of its owner, and it will stop working when this person dies. The belief is represented in this turn of the century French drawing

announce his entry into the place to collect a soul. The sound of two bells in a house ringing for no reason also presages a death, although church bells are believed to be able to drive away evil spirits and if they are rung during a storm will cause the fury of the weather to abate.

In quite a few places, America in particular, it is claimed that a clock will stop when its owner dies, as the words of that famous song, 'Grandfather's Clock', have immortalized:

Ninety years without slumbering,
His life's seconds numbering,
But it stopped short, never to go again,
When the old man died.

The reason for this comparatively recent superstition having developed is not hard to discover, for earlier models of clocks were operated by mechanisms which required specific and regular attention. In most cases, of course, it was probably only the owner who knew how to carry out such a task, and if he was laid up in his final illness this would clearly not get done. So as he 'wound down' so would his clock, the two of them quite likely coming to a stop at the same time. Any clock which chimes out of sequence is indicating a death in the household, and one which suddenly goes faster or strikes thirteen times is equally ominous. Items of furniture acting in strange ways, such as creaking inexplicably or falling over for no apparent reason, are also omens of death, while any picture falling from a wall (or mirror for that matter) in a sick-room warns that the person who is ill does not have long to live.

In certain rural areas of Europe it is still held that a person who is about to die is somehow gifted with powers of prophecy. This is another very old idea and might well be explained by the verse in the Bible in *Genesis* (chapter 49, verses 2 and 33) when Jacob summons his sons and says: 'Gather yourselves together, that I may tell you that which shall befall you in the last days. And when Jacob had made an end of commanding his sons, he gathered up his feet into the bed and yielded up the ghost, and was gathered unto his people.' Shakespeare is one among many writers who knew of this belief, and he refers to it in both *Richard II* and *Henry IV*.

The actual moment of dying is also the subject of a number of specific beliefs, as Willard A. Heaps reports in his book, *Superstition* (1972):

The eyes should immediately be closed by someone present while the body is still warm. It is thought that if they are left open, the deceased person will look for someone to join him in death. A coin, which could be used in future life, was often placed on each eye. However, this act was a practical one, so that the undertaker would not have difficulty in closing

It is tempting fate to sit in a coffin, even in fun, according to an old belief. Ray Milland, however, seems to be unaffected in this still from the film *The Premature Burial* (1962)

the eyelids after they had stiffened. Pulling a sheet over the head is a throwback to the time when bodies were buried in shrouds rather than clothes.

To these I might just add the British belief that if a corpse remains warm after the usual period in which it grows cold, this is an omen of another death in the same family.

The custom of ringing a church bell after someone's death is partly rooted in superstition, for aside from honouring the deceased it also drove off evil spirits, as Francis Grose has explained in his *Antiquities of England and Wales* (1773–87):

It was anciently rung for two purposes; one to bespeak the prayers of all good Christians for a soul just departing; the other to drive away the evil spirits who stood at the bed's foot and about the house, ready to seize their prey or at least to molest and terrify the soul in its passing.

In many parts of the British Isles and Europe the custom also developed of watching over the corpse after death so that it was not carried off by spirits; with the passage of time this practice developed into the 'wake', which became more of a celebration than a watch.

The funeral service itself has not avoided the attention of superstition, and you would be well advised never to let anyone lie or sit in a coffin – even for fun; the Germans believe this is inviting death to take you. It is, though, lucky to kiss or touch the body of someone who has died, for this shows there is no ill-will between you and will prevent the deceased from later haunting you. The wearing of black is partly in deference to the very old idea that it disguised a person so that they could not be recognized and haunted by the ghost of the person who had died (accentuated by women wearing veils), and equally because, as the colour of night,

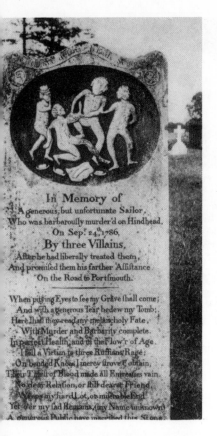

In Memory of
A generous, but unfortunate Sailor,
Who was barbarously murder'd on Hindhead,
On Sep.r 24.th 1786,
By three Villains,
After he had liberally treated them,
And promised them his farther Affiftance
On the Road to Portfmouth.

When pitying Eyes to fee my Grave fhall come;
And with a generous Tear bedew my Tomb;
Here fhall they read any melancholy Fate;
With Murder and Barbarity complete.
In perfect Health, and in the Flow'r of Age,
I fall a Victim to three Ruffians Rage;
On bended Knees I mercy ftrove t'obtain,
Their Thirft of Blood made all Entreaties vain.
No dear Relation, or ftill dearer Friend,
Weeps my hard Lot, or miferable End.
Yet o'er my fad Remains, (my Name unknown)
A generous Public have inscribed this Stone.

Graveyards and cemeteries have been the subject of numerous superstitions, and originally tombstones were decorated to keep away evil spirits

A modern practitioner of *Wicca* carrying out a ritual ceremony. This lady is continuing a tradition that goes back to pagan times

it showed a person's abandonment to grief. The journey of the coffin to its burial should not be interrupted as this apparently gives the deceased's spirit a chance to escape and maybe return as a ghost.

Superstition is not right, I am afraid, when it claims that any land a corpse is carried over becomes a public right of way (there have been several legal rulings to this effect in the past when the belief has been put into practice), nor does there seem to be much evidence that any field a coffin is carried over thereafter only yields poor crops. While good manners would seem to insist that any man should remove his hat out of respect when a cortège passes, superstition holds out a death warning to the man who ignores the custom. Not so many years ago anyone who was passed by such a procession was supposed to bare his head and then walk a few paces with the coffin to avoid this fate.

Superstition has not yet had time to get to work on the crematorium, but graveyards have always been the subject of some strange beliefs. The reason for the south side of the church being regarded as the holiest and the place where people insisted on being buried was because of the old idea that the south wind carried corruption. Only those who had not been baptized, had committed suicide or been convicted of murder were placed on the north side. (Any people who it was considered had led evil lives might well be buried at cross-roads – because of the magical power of the cross in any form – or at least staked with large iron nails to prevent them rising as ghosts.) Tradition says graves should be dug in an east to west direction, so that a body may lie with its head to the west and be ready to rise when the call comes on Judgement Day.

It is easy to understand why it is considered ominous if there is any difficulty in placing a coffin in the ground; superstition tells us this occurs because the soul of the deceased is making a last attempt to escape. The placing of wreaths on the grave is a variation of the old custom of putting there gifts of food and precious objects to appease the ghosts, although because of the special power of certain flowers the action is also said to prevent any evil spirits getting into the coffin. It has been suggested that the first tombstones were placed on graves to keep the dead *in*, but it seems more likely that as primitive man believed spirits could dwell in stones, these markers were placed at the graveside so the spirit of the dead person might dwell in peace there and not trouble the living. To rob a grave has always been considered very ill-omened, although it did not put a stop to the body snatchers, or resurrection men, of old, and indeed there have been some very unpleasant

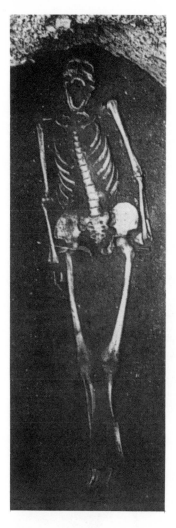

The body of a suspected witch found in the Essex village of St Osyth in 1921. The unhappy person had been buried in the manner decreed by superstition – with rivets through the thigh bones, knees and feet to prevent the corpse from rising later

instances of it happening only recently with the stealing of the bodies of film producer Mike Todd in 1977, and that of the great comedian Charlie Chaplin a year later. One might well hope that ghouls who could do such things *were* haunted by the malevolent ghosts superstition says their actions set free.

Speaking of such men, who have inspired universal revulsion, brings me conveniently on to the topic of witches, whose activities over the centuries have inspired many of the superstitions I have noted in these pages, particularly those to do with sickness and death. The whole subject of witchcraft is an enormous and complex one which has given rise to many hundreds of books, and it is not my intention here to enter into any kind of detailed discussion about it: there just is not enough space and there are many more qualified than I who have written informed books on the subject.

Witches and warlocks (the term for a male witch) fall into two distinct categories, those who practise 'black' or evil magic and those who work 'white' or good magic. Both are, of course, rooted in the supernatural, though the real white witchcraft, or *Wicca* as it is known, is an ancient fertility religion which can be traced back to the days of very early man. The working of black magic, the worshipping of the supreme evil being, the Devil, through diabolism and degeneration, is certainly a very old idea, too, but it is doubtful whether it has been an organized practice until comparatively modern times. The followers of *Wicca* believed in the gods of Nature and sought their aid to ensure fertility for man, his beasts and crops; good health and happiness for themselves; and the ability to work simple cures for those who came to them for help. Such people, often referred to as 'witch doctors' or 'cunning' men and women, have functioned on the edge of society over the centuries, and indeed still do to this day. The black witches whose purpose has been self-aggrandizement, sexual excesses, and the working of evil spells and cures against enemies real or imagined have been very much in the minority and concealed themselves in great secrecy. This said, the terrible persecution of people accused of being witches during medieval and later times was carried out almost wholly under the sanction of the churches to support their own authority, and based on charges more often than not fraudulent and mostly cast by people out of jealousy and malice.

The Devil has always been seen as the head of the witches, and invariably those said to belong to his ranks summoned him by way of complex ritual, and he appeared either in person or in the shape of demons or familiars – tiny creatures who in drawings bear an uncanny resemblance to farm animals and domestic pets and

Superstition at work today – an eye being painted on the door of a home to keep evil spirits at bay

almost certainly were – and in this way was his dark work done amongst us. Because the Evil One had such a central place in the fears of mankind and his influence was seen in all manner of disasters, in death, disease and misfortune, it is not surprising that practices based on superstition developed to counter his machinations and those of his emissaries, the witches. Although people feared the activities of the demons or familiars they believed all witches had at their command, they were much more afraid of the Evil Eye. Every witch was said to be able to 'overlook' any man, woman, child or creature, and by so doing cause them to fall temporarily ill or even to die. Many, then, were the devices

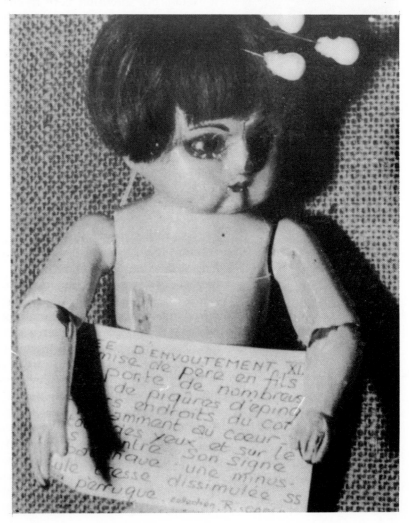

A witch 'poppet' found in France that had been used in an attempt to 'spell' someone to death

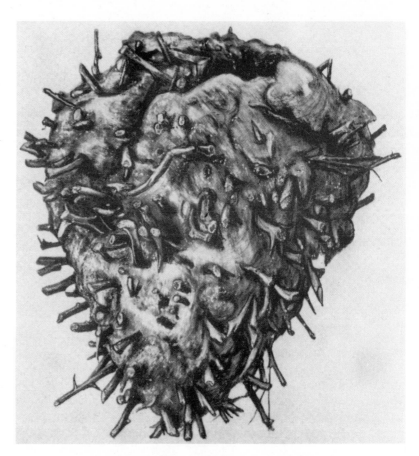

Another of the grisly devices used in witchcraft to try and kill someone by a curse. This is a calf's heart which has been stuck with pins and thorns

constructed by man to avoid this Evil Eye. For example, witches were said to be averse to iron objects (hence the popularity of the horseshoe), could be driven away by spitting at them, or prevented from entering a house by hanging sprigs of leaves from such revered trees as the elder, the bay, the laurel, and, of course, the holly bush. The most effective form of protection, however, was said to be a picture of the sacred Egyptian 'Eye of Osiris' painted on the doors or wall of a house – or on the prow of a boat for that matter – and the photograph reproduced here is typical of many found all over the world. Superstition also claims that anyone with different coloured eyes, or eyes set very close together, may well have the Evil Eye whether they are a witch or not, and that the custom of blackening the eyebrows and putting shadow on the eyelids was originally done as a charm against the Evil Eye.

Witches of all kinds were popularly believed to have the power to work spells or put curses on people, and a kind of minor industry grew up around these. Because of the nature of spells, the practising witch could apparently have it both ways, for when someone was 'spelled' they might well go to the witch who had placed it on an enemy's behalf and pay them to reverse the process. The most widely used methods of casting such spells were either to make a small wax or clay model of the person to be 'spelled' (it was

Illustration from an anonymous work, *Secrets of Magic*, published in France in 1920 showing the sign made by magicians to ward off any death spell directed at them

supposed to be particularly effective if a few strands of the person's hair or nail clippings could be incorporated), or else to use the heart of a calf or sheep. Into both of these pins or thorns had to be pushed and at the same time the following words recited:

It is not this heart I mean to burn,
But the person's heart I wish to turn,
Wishing them neither rest nor peace
Till they are dead and gone.

Once this was accomplished the 'poppet' (as the figures were sometimes called) or pierced heart had to be hidden away as close to where the victim lived as possible. It is interesting to note that such spells are apparently most used during periods of war and there were a particularly large number of instances reported during the First World War, directed against the enemy and among people who had developed irrational hatred of their neighbours. There was also a flourishing traffic in a letter which was supposed to protect the owner against witchcraft, both men away at the war (they were, of course, believed to be fighting the forces of Satan) and those at home. It read:

In the name of the Father and of the Son and of the Holy Ghost, Amen. And in the name of our Lord Jesus Christ. I will give thee protection and will give relief to thy creatures, thy cows, calves, horses, sheep and pigs, and all creatures that alive be in thy possession from all witchcraft and from all other assaults of Satan. Amen.

Children have always been thought to be particularly vulnerable to the attacks of witches, before their birth as well as after. Superstition tells us that it is most important that a pregnant mother's craving for any strange food should always be satisfied, as there are witches around who will readily offer this food in return for being allowed to bring the child-to-be up in the ways of witchcraft. For generations, birthmarks were thought to be the mark of the Devil – many people of all ages were branded as witches on just such evidence – and many bizarre methods were developed to try and get rid of them. Of course, the young baby was in danger of witchcraft until he had been baptized, and when in his cradle should be protected either with a knife or some other iron object, or else a Holy Communion wafer, as Robert Herrick advises in his *Hesperides* (1648):

Bring the holy crust of bread,
Lay it underneath the head;
'Tis a certain charm to keep
Hags away while children sleep.

Even though many of the actions put down to witchcraft seem absurd and quite impossible to us in the later part of the twentieth

Practitioners of Voodoo use many elements of superstition and magic in their rituals, as this photograph taken at a gathering on Haiti shows

■ A grave matter: In Haiti a man on a murder charge has been granted an adjournment of his trial until August 1 —to give him the time he wants to resurrect the victim and call him as a defence witness.

An indication of just how seriously Voodoo is taken in Haiti – a newspaper cutting from *The Daily Mirror*, 25 June 1973

The modern witch doctor in Africa has a respected place in both the village and the town, and some of his abilities, which have always been treated as superstitions, are now being taken much more seriously

century, it would be wrong to think that either black or white magic were things of the past. There are small groups of people practising the ancient customs of *Wicca* throughout Britain, Europe and America, just as there are those following the perverted path of Devil Worship and Satanism. (The twentieth century's most famous witchcraft leader was certainly Dr Gerald Gardner who ran a network of covens all over Britain; while Aleister Crowley 'the Great Beast' was the century's leading black magician.) The very fact that man is still inherently superstitious clearly has much to do with this, and recently Dr Gustav Jahoda, of the Department of Psychology at the University of Strathclyde in Glasgow, noted just how strong a part the concepts of witchcraft continue to play in western society. After conducting a survey among a group of students he reported in *Nature* (December 1968) that of 280 male students who answered a questionnaire, 116 stated

OFFICIAL STATUS URGED FOR WITCH DOCTORS

By Our Geneva Correspondent

African governments are to be recommended to make "definite political decisions" to encourage the development of traditional medicine as practised by healers such as witch-doctors and herbalists, the World Health Organisation said yesterday in Geneva.

This was the conclusion of a World Health Organisation regional expert committee meeting in Brazzaville, Congo. Traditional healers should be integrated into government health teams, while other health workers should be trained in traditional medicine, the experts considered.

While most Africans believe in traditional medicine, it is often the only source of care in rural areas far away from modern health centres.

Confirmation of the changing attitude towards the African witch doctor – a report from *The Daily Telegraph*, 10 March 1976

MODERN PROVERB : Never carve up a funeral cortege. An impatient driver tried to squeeze between cars heading for a Long Island interment and caused an eight-vehicle collision that injured 14 mourners. 'I thought we'd all end up buried,' the late lamented's sister commented bitterly.

Coincidental with my finishing this book, yet another old superstition was shown to be still alive and flourishing. Or undead would perhaps be more accurate! From *The Daily Mail*, Friday, 13 October 1978

that 'witchcraft as a power' probably does exist, while 98 affirmed that it 'certainly does exist'; only 27 stated that witchcraft 'probably does not exist', while there were 39 sceptics who said 'it certainly does not exist'. From his survey, Dr Jahoda concluded that 'there was no evidence that either university education in general or any particular type of course, including scientific training, has any discernible impact on the magico-mythical beliefs entertained by the students'.

Nor does the evidence end there, for in Africa, which has been dominated by the power of witchcraft for centuries, there is no denying that witch doctors still hold sway over enormous numbers of people. There is evidence, too, that this hold extends even to other parts of the world where Africans have emigrated. Indeed such is the importance of the role of witchcraft in the societies of certain African countries, that recently moves were announced to give official status to witch doctors! And Voodoo, that strange mixture of witchcraft and Christianity which is very much part of life in Brazil and Haiti, not to mention parts of America, is also accepted as having a relevance to modern living. Like witchcraft in all its forms, it too is rooted in curious ancient lore and superstition.

Such revelations can only make one wonder if superstition itself is going to achieve some form of official sanction in the fullness of time? We may try to deny its existence, yet at every turn, consciously or unconsciously, we pay heed to factors we learned in childhood and, come what may, will carry to our graves. Despite the many superstitions that we can now explain and even rationalize, there are many more that defy our logic: yet can we throw them off? The very existence of this book is emphatic proof we cannot. And as a superstitious man myself – much as I would like not to be – I am sure we shall continue to perpetuate this extraordinary element of our being just as those before us have done, being reminded all the time of those lines of the anonymous old sage who wrote:

How superstitiously we mind our evils!
The throwing down of salt, or crossing of a hare,
Bleeding at nose, the stumbling of a horse
Or singing of a cricket, are of power
To daunt the whole man in us.

INDEX